Praise for *The Es*

"A sure winner! *The Essential Wooden* presents the basics of leadership as taught by one of America's great leaders, John Wooden. His observations and conclusions about success and competitive greatness are as brilliant as gems—and just as valuable."

> —KEN BLANCHARD, coauthor of
> *The One Minute Manager*® and
> *Leading at a Higher Level*

"*The Essential Wooden* is vintage Coach Wooden and a great book for all managers who want to become more effective. Coach Wooden's values and methods will lead to lasting, positive results."

> —JEFF HENLEY, Vice Chairman of the Board,
> Oracle Corporation

"It has been my privilege to have several conversations with John Wooden. Every time I learn and grow from that experience. It is now your turn to receive nuggets of wisdom from this wonderful teacher. Each page of *The Essential Wooden* will benefit you and your organization."

> —JOHN C. MAXWELL, author, speaker, and
> founder INJOY Stewardship Services and EQUIP

"A wonderful exposition of commonsense leadership from an uncommon leader—John Wooden. His legendary achievements stem from his 'old-fashioned' values. In *The Essential Wooden* he reveals how his character and skills were honed and how they apply in the twenty-first century. Required reading for anyone who aspires to being a great leader."

—STEPHEN R. COVEY, author,
The 7 Habits of Highly Effective People and
The 8th Habit: From Effectiveness to Greatness

THE
ESSENTIAL
WOODEN

THE ESSENTIAL

A Lifetime of Lessons on
Leaders and Leadership

JOHN WOODEN
AND STEVE JAMISON

NEW YORK   CHICAGO   SAN FRANCISCO   ATHENS
LONDON   MADRID   MEXICO CITY   MILAN
NEW DELHI   SINGAPORE   SYDNEY   TORONTO

1 2 3 4 5 6 7 8 9 QFR 23 22 21 20 19 18

ISBN   978-1-260-12910-6
MHID   1-260-12910-1

e-ISBN   978-1-260-12909-0
e-MHID   1-260-12909-8

McGraw-Hill Education books are available at special quantity discounts to use as premiums and sales promotions, or for use in corporate training programs. To contact a representative, please visit the Contact Us page at www.mhprofessional.com.

Interior design by Lee Fukui and Mauna Eichner.

Appreciation to our editor, Jeffrey Krames, for sharing his great knowledge and to Ruth Mannino for guidance on design and editorial production.

Photo credits:

page ii: Frank Oliver, Journal and Courier (Lafayette, Indiana)

pages 1, 53, 135: Richard Clarkson

page 101: AP Worldwide Photos

This book is dedicated to those I have been privileged to serve as teacher, coach, and leader.

For Jim and Nan—Nell's and my son and daughter—and our 20 additional blessings: 7 grandchildren and 13 great-grandchildren.

And for Nell, whom I miss every single day.

—John Wooden

For Mary Jean and Ev Edstrom, my parents, and my four intelligent (and very beautiful) sisters—Pat, Kris, Kate, and Kim. And for John Wooden—thank you for your trust.

—Steve Jamison

CONTENTS

viii

**THE
ESSENTIAL
WOODEN**

FOREWORD

by Judy Olian
Dean of UCLA Anderson School of Management
and John E. Anderson Chair in Management

I first met John Wooden about 11 years ago at his Encino apartment in Los Angeles, a modest abode stacked floor to ceiling with books, awards, mementos from admirers, and artifacts of his unrivaled career. The simple apartment preserved the exact furnishings that had been chosen and placed by his beloved wife Nellie, who died in 1985. It had become a lot more crowded because of all that had transpired in Coach's life since her passing—the books he had authored, and the symbols of his revered stature bestowed upon him by admirers from all walks of life, from US presidents to spiritual, athletic, and business leaders to average citizens whose lives he had profoundly touched.

One had to be small to fit into that apartment, and in his advanced years, Coach Wooden's humility seemed to shrink him, notwithstanding his outsized reputation. Despite the admiration he garnered from so many famous athletes and leaders across the spectrum, there were no trappings of celebrity around him. He didn't seem particularly impressed with his awards and possessions. For him, success was measured in what he could do for others.

Initially, I was perplexed by the impact he had—not just on his players who carried his lessons for the rest of their lives, or on coaches who marveled at his brilliance in transforming teams into winning machines—but on the many people who felt he had helped them become better versions of themselves. I came to appreciate the parallels that so many saw—between the "School of Wooden" on the court, and the direct transfer of those principles to leadership and honorable living, anywhere.

His impact wasn't just on those around UCLA who knew him personally, or knew about him. He was a source of proven wisdom on how to lead teams and organizations to a common goal, a strategist whose preparation for athletic competition applied also to readiness to compete in markets or to inspire community organizations, a role model whose values served as a touchstone of how to live with integrity and purpose.

Coach developed his principles on the basketball court. And yet, to me, it's remarkable how well they apply to business. "Keeping it simple" is brilliant strategic advice. Complexity is difficult to communicate and often confuses organizations. "Pay attention to the basics"—for Coach it was shoes, shoelaces, and socks that are literally the grounding for any player. For businesses it's how you sweat the small details—that's the essential building block of great companies.

Coach Wooden was famous for being a man of few words. He seemed to coach little during the games themselves, even during the most crucial tournaments. Watching replays of his games reminded me of legendary conductor Leonard Bernstein. When guiding his beloved New York Philharmonic orchestra, Bernstein was known to cross his arms, tuck his baton away, and watch with joy as the orchestra directed itself. Of course, Wooden's teams, and Bernstein's musicians, were masters, trained to perfection. Coach's teams were fitter than any others—they could outrun, outplay, and outlast their competitors. They had honed their craft through intense and meticulous preparation under the watchful eye of Coach. When his team came to play in actual competition, players were ready and knew the drill like a finely tuned machine. Coach pulled back and didn't need to hover—the team already knew what to do. That's the mark of a great leader in an organization.

Here's another piece of advice that transcends the basketball court: "Treat everyone fairly, but not equally"—that's tricky advice in today's sometimes politicized cultures, yet it's so astute. Individuals differ in their needs, in how they absorb feedback or respond to suggestions, in the self-confidence or insecurities they bring to the court or to the office, in the balance of skills or hidden talents they possess. A leader must adapt to that complex package of individual differences to draw out the best in each team member, on or off the court. Coach did that by tailoring his motivation techniques—fairly but not necessarily equally—to the needs of each player, just as a good leader should do.

Over time, these values, at the heart of Coach's Pyramid of Success, became part of our leadership ethos at UCLA Anderson School of Management. Positioning graduates to lead and to lead significant lives is core to our mission, and we've embraced Coach's values in our leadership training.

When I met Coach, he was 96. By then he was celebrated not just as an iconic basketball coach with an unrivaled championship record, but also as a life teacher who lived by his principles with integrity and authenticity. As he considered his legacy, he felt it needed to center on his teachings—about looking inward to be the best *you* can be, about focusing on life events you control, about working toward common purpose. Coach wanted those learnings to continue in a program, and through role models who embodied those principles. So he was a strong supporter of the creation of the Wooden Awards at UCLA Anderson. And to this day, we select a global leader and several students, who embody the values-based principles of Coach Wooden's Pyramid of Success, to receive this prestigious award each year.

As I read through this book, I was reminded of the pleasure of hearing Coach Wooden speak, of his charming aphorisms and poetry, about how to live and lead. We're entrusted to keep that part of his legacy alive. Better yet, beyond bestowing awards to others, let's try to live our own lives by his principles.

PREFACE

by Steve Jamison

⇒ PLAY TO WIN ⇐

The year is 2005. Seated across from John Wooden in the den of the home where he lived for more than three decades, one can suddenly—unexpectedly—discern in his eyes the cold, calculating look of a lion measuring its prey: "We play to win," he told me in a flat, hard tone. "Do I have to tell people that we play to win?"

There was annoyance in his voice—then more stern: "I wanted to win every single game I ever played or coached. Who would think otherwise? We play to win." And John Wooden did.

Without warning, the great competitive fire of one of the greatest team builders and competitors in the history of American sports has revealed itself. At 95 years old—the lion in the late winter—he could still send a chill down your spine when he fixed that predatory look of a cold-blooded competitor upon you.

Then he addressed an additional concern, namely, that "We play to win" will be misinterpreted or otherwise distorted: "Steve, they must understand that while

I played to win—*always*—winning was never the way I measured my success. Nor was it how I gauged the success of those under my supervision."

He paused, then issued a summary statement of clarification: "For me there is a standard that ranks above winning. I would never allow the scoreboard to be the judge of whether I had achieved success."

That scoreboard, as you know, smiled down on Coach Wooden's UCLA basketball teams more often than not: 10 March Madness national championships in 12 years; 7 national championships in a row; an 88-game winning streak; a 38-game winning streak in national championship tournament play; 12 Final Four appearances in 14 years; 4 "perfect" seasons. All these records will probably still be intact 100 or 500 years from now.

Teams under John Wooden's supervision endured just one season that produced a losing record. It was his first year as a coach back at Dayton, Kentucky—the Greendevils—in 1932–1933. Never again in the four decades that followed was there a losing season.

Yet all this spectacular production—*winning*—came from a leader and master team builder *who never ever mentioned that word to his teams*. Why? He wanted their complete focus on the higher standard, the one that means even more to him than winning.

That begs this question: "Hey, what can possibly mean more than winning?" To give you an answer, let me offer an insight from a collaboration of more than 10 years with Coach Wooden that led to bestsellers (*Wooden*, *Wooden on Leadership*, and others), our award-winning PBS presentation, *Wooden: Values, Victory, and Peace of Mind*, an acclaimed website, coachwooden.com, and a movie about his life.

⇥ Effort Is Paramount ⇤

Early in his career, John Wooden embraced the belief that success, as measured by each one of us individually, is the peace of mind derived from making the absolute and complete *effort* to do the best of which you are capable. The quality of your effort to realize your potential counts first and foremost.

For John Wooden *that* is success. And it is different from winning—beating an opponent in basketball, business, or life.

This is important to recognize: that *success* and *winning* are two very different concepts in the world of Wooden and that success is the foremost of the two. Eddie Powell, a former assistant coach and player, observed, "Coach Wooden was more upset if we won but *didn't* work up to our potential than if we lost playing at our best."

That represents a radically different approach to leadership—a universe apart from "winning is the only thing" or "winning at any cost" or "Just win, baby!"

And yet John Wooden wanted very much to win "every *single* game." This, of course, is an apparent contradiction in belief and behavior; specifically, Coach Wooden's fierce competitive instinct and desire to win coupled with his deep and abiding conviction that success, as he defined it, supersedes (and often precedes) victory.

Reconciling the two is challenging—to seek winning with all you've got and yet not allow it to be the arbiter of whether you succeed. Nevertheless, to fully appreciate John Wooden's approach to competition, team building, and leadership, you must grasp the fact that he was able to simultaneously and ferociously "play to win" and yet *not* allow the results—the score, trophies, titles, or championships—to be the ultimate measure of his own or his team's success.

That's the subject of this book: how he was able to teach his teams to win by teaching them to believe in a standard even higher than victory. Therein, perhaps, lies the leadership genius of John Robert Wooden, a leader whose teams won over and over and over again but who never mentioned winning.

Included in *The Essential Wooden* are key insights from former players and managers—not only those who were part of the UCLA dynasty but also those who go all the way back to Coach Wooden's earliest days as a leader. Throughout the decades, a common theme appears in their opinions: John Wooden was a man of character who cared deeply about the people he taught.

His former players are the first in line to attest to his character. And the words and phrases they use include "demanding," "honest," "strong-willed," "professional," "caring," "driven," "respectful," "principled," "sincere," "determined," "a gentleman," "precise," "energetic," "moral," "organized," "a pistol," "unrelenting," "gracious," "deliberative," "competitive," "disciplined," "intelligent," "balance," "work ethic," "a pioneer," "fun," "fierce," "positive," "patient," "persistent," "fair," and "loyal."

Were there complaints about Coach Wooden? Of course. Players who weren't in the starting lineup were not always happy; many complained. A few were bitter about bench duty but nevertheless adhered to the system John Wooden created. This is the mark of an extraordinary leader.

John Wooden fought hard to win, and his players did the same. However, early on he had been taught by his father, Joshua Hugh Wooden, that a more important contest—one beyond winning—was going on inside each of us. It was the struggle, the effort, we make "to be the best *you* can be."

You might find it easy to pay lip service to this concept, but it is most difficult to fully embrace it—to truly believe that the quality of your effort is the first measure of success, not the final score, promotion, salary, or all the rest. It is *difficult* but not impossible.

John Wooden did it, and it's a fundamental component of why he became one of the greatest winners of the twentieth century. He was resolute in his devotion to what his father taught him about success.

As a leader, John Wooden had double vision; that is, he had a microscope in one eye and a telescope in the other. Out on the distant horizon where he focused the telescope, he saw perfection in performance and execution. Up close, under the microscope, he saw the prerequisite details for achieving that personal perfection he called *competitive greatness*.

What was in between? The step-by-step blueprint he created for reaching that far horizon: his Pyramid of Success. All of this and more constitute *The Essential Wooden*, the philosophy and methodology of a master teacher, consummate coach, and legendary leader.

INTRODUCTION TO THE PAPERBACK EDITION

John Wooden:
A Master Beyond Basketball

by Steve Jamison

Good leadership is most readily apparent in sports. So is bad leadership. In fact, judging the merits, good, bad, and otherwise, of leaders in sports is a national sport itself. And in the judgment of most, when it comes to leadership John Wooden was a master.

While the context and specifics of leadership vary from sports to business, one fundamental challenge is exactly the same: specifically, managing a group of individuals so they work together at their highest level in pursuit of a common objective, whether it's a quarterly goal or a field goal in the fourth quarter.

In this regard, John Wooden set the gold standard for leadership. His ability to transform a vastly disparate group of individuals into a single-minded team able to perform with competitive greatness under the greatest pressure is legendary. The record book bulges with his astounding and nearly incomprehensible achievements: 10 March Madness national championships in 12 seasons—7 of them in consecutive years; 4 *perfect* seasons; 88 victories in a row; 38 straight victories in March Madness tournament play. And more. It is not an overstatement to say these records will never be broken. Coach Wooden put up pretty good numbers.

The Essential Wooden is a deep dig by the legendary coach into how he did it and what lessons you can draw for yourself and your own business team.

But here's a most important fact and the starting point for John Wooden and his concept of leadership success: He did not judge himself by those outrageous numbers, but rather on what went into making them happen, namely, the quality and intensity of effort and intelligence he put forth as a coach, teacher, and leader trying to build a team that lived up to its potential in achieving competitive greatness.

That's how he kept score—the *quality of his effort* as a leader, and he did not look for his final grade in the sports pages or up on the scoreboard. "Only I knew if I was a success," he wrote. John Wooden did not allow others to grant him success—not his boss, UCLA athletic director J.D. Morgan, not the chancellor of UCLA, not the fans, alumni, or media. Only he knew. Only he could grant success to himself because only he truly understood if he had applied the equivalent of a full court press on himself in the area of leadership.

Coach Wooden believed the same applies to you: only you truly know if you are a success in doing absolutely all you can—a personal full court press—to lead your team to competitive greatness. As he wrote, "Talent to spare, or spare on talent, a leader's goal remains the same, namely, getting the very best out of the people in your organization." How he accomplished that is the essence of *The Essential Wooden*.

Never a losing season while coaching 27 years at UCLA, John Wooden was a master when it came to maximizing individual and combined ability regardless of the level of talent on his teams. He had something that was near-genius in his understanding and teaching of the nuts and bolts of basketball, but even more important he understood human nature and how to forge individuals into a formidable competitive group.

Whether he was coaching a superstar like Kareem Abdul-Jabbar or Bill Walton, or lesser known student-athletes like Grover Luchsinger (1948–1949) or Cortland Borio (1952–1954), he was driven by the same fierce objective: teaching Kareem, Bill, Grover, Cortland, and all the others to be the best they could be in ways that served their *team* best. In this endeavor he applied extraordinary skills, many of which are directly applicable to you and your own leadership and managerial objectives.

In the pages that follow, Coach Wooden shares his secrets to success, although he didn't consider them secrets. In fact, if you asked him what he did to bring about competitive greatness he would have been happy to sit down over a glazed donut and a glass of iced tea and tell you. That conversation, as I learned myself, could take years.

From our talks over those years here are John Wooden's hand-picked selection of directives and opinions, illustrative stories and observations on leadership that are enlightening and practical, suggestions you can put to work in your own leadership and management efforts *today*.

Added to his own keen analysis are opinions and conclusions of many of his former players and assistant coaches who bring supporting data to what Coach Wooden revealed here.

As he told me long ago, "There is nothing fancy about what I teach about team building, nothing that requires a special gift, privilege, or access to power."

In fact, one of the skills he acquired over his decades of teaching and coaching and leadership (they were the same thing in his mind) was the ability to distill—simplify—the essence of ideas into potent maxims and axioms: "Don't mistake activity for achievement." "When I am through learning I am through." "Be slow to criticize and quick to commend." "Don't let yesterday take up too much of today." And there are many more in these pages.

Of course, there's more to mastery than maxims and *The Essential Wooden* delves into it with clarity and substance.

To invoke an old joke, if you look up the meaning of "winner" in the dictionary you'll find a picture of John Wooden. To stretch the joke a bit more, if you look up the meaning of champion, legend, or leader you'll see the same picture although the picture next to leader will be the largest.

Of course, his image is not in the dictionary (yet) but it's on the cover of this book. I find that looking at it reveals the essence of perhaps the greatest leader, teacher, and coach of the twentieth century.

Look at that photograph for a moment and let it be your starting point for a journey into the core of great leadership as taught by John Wooden.

PROLOGUE

For more than 10 years I have worked with Steve Jamison in a most productive collaboration designed to share publicly my philosophy of success and how to achieve it. I'm extremely pleased with our results. His understanding of my overall philosophy and methodology—what I did as a leader and why I did it— is comprehensive, and he has a terrific ability to articulate that knowledge.

The Essential Wooden continues our collaboration and expands on the themes presented in *Wooden on Leadership*.

There is nothing fancy in what I teach about team building—nothing that requires a special gift, privilege, or access to power. Rather, it requires dedication to certain principles and concepts that I include in this book.

First and foremost is my belief that success is within the grasp of each and every one of us. *Success*, as I define it, is not determined by fame, fortune, or being number 1. Of course, this is heresy for many leaders—to suggest that something could be more important than being number 1.

Over and over I have taught those under my supervision that we are all given a certain potential *unique* to each one of us. Our first responsibility is to make the utmost effort to bring forth that potential in service to our team. For me, that is success.

Then perhaps when circumstances come together, we may find ourselves number 1. If that happens, it is merely a by-product of the effort we make to realize our own competency—our full potential. Success may result in winning, but winning does not necessarily mean you are a success. I also believe it is harmful to compare yourself to others—to judge your own success based on how you stack up against someone else. Others will do that for you. My approach is to judge myself—and those under my supervision—on the effort we make to become our best as a team.

Of course, in the twenty-first century it seems that comparing oneself to others and worrying about being number 1 are national and corporate obsessions.

If that's your approach, fine. But for me, it wasn't fine. I did it another way, and this book shares the essentials of my style—the philosophy and methodology of my leadership. I sincerely hope you find there a few ideas that you can put to good use with your own organization.

PART I

LEADERSHIP, VALUES, VICTORY, AND SUCCESS

PRESEASON LETTER TO THE TEAM

If each of you makes every effort to develop to the best of your ability, follow the proper rules of conduct and activity most conducive to good physical condition, subordinate individual acclaim for the welfare of the team, and permit no personality clashes or differences of opinion with teammates or coaches to interfere with your or a teammate's efforts, it will be a very rewarding year.

⇥ Who I Am ⇤

I am a lucky man—a teacher. I believe that teaching may be the most rewarding job on earth. Perhaps the most important next to being a parent.

What follows is my philosophy of leadership, my concept of success and how to achieve it, and my approach to coaching (which is another word for "team building"). I've spent most of my professional life teaching all three. All three are bound together as essential elements of my overall system.

In his dictionary, Mr. Webster's definition of what a teacher does is illuminating: giving "instruction and guidance with a specific end in mind until rapid and *successful execution* of assigned duties and tasks is assured."

For four decades, I tried to accomplish this as a leader and coach who taught members of the team how to successfully execute their assigned roles and responsibilities at the uppermost level of their abilities in ways that best serve the group.

Regardless of the profession, all good leaders strive for this same result, and I've never met one worth his or her salt who wasn't a good teacher.

⇥ Leadership's Greatest Reward ⇤

Mr. Webster fails to mention that during the process of being a teacher, coach, and leader, something extraordinary can occur: You will actually create an honest-to-goodness team, its members joined in a way comparable only to being in a strong family with bonds that last a lifetime.

That is what I love so dearly about leadership. Over and over again it allowed me the privilege of building and being part of that special family we call "a team," a group of individuals striving to achieve competitive greatness and success. I am a lucky man.

⇥ THE PREREQUISITE FOR LEADERSHIP ⇤

These words are worth consideration. They go straight to the core of a being an effective leader: "Live as though you'll die tomorrow. *Learn* as though you'll live forever."

The words convey a fitting sense of energy and urgency. Don't squander a single day, and seek knowledge as if you will never die. It is an instruction on how to be an enlightened leader—one who lasts.

Longevity in leadership is related, in part, to your love of learning and the sense of urgency you attach to it.

⇥ LEADERS NEVER STOP LEARNING ⇤

Ben Franklin made this observation about a fellow he had known in Philadelphia: "The man died at 25, but wasn't buried until 75." Mr. Franklin was describing a man who stopped learning early on.

In my field of work the leader is called "a coach." To excel as a coach and leader, you must be a good teacher; to excel as a teacher, leader, and coach, you must remain a student who keeps learning. You must not die at 25.

I believe the key to learning is listening with both your ears and your eyes. For me, it happened gradually, but it happened because I was blessed with teachers worth listening to.

A Compass for Character

We play to win, of course, but what happens prior to the final score is even more important. Whatever I did as a leader, teacher, and coach started with one man: Joshua Hugh Wooden. He has been my compass in leadership and life—the person who taught me about the final score and what precedes *and* supersedes it.

My father was a remarkable person. In large part self-schooled (just like Abe Lincoln), he was drawn to the classics in literature and poetry. He had keen intelligence, common sense, and resilient physical and emotional strength. Dad possessed a near-photographic memory. I still smile when I remember him sitting in the kitchen working on a crossword puzzle—in ink. Rarely did he make a mistake.

He also had a practical kind of wisdom. For example, he constantly reminded his four young sons to abide by what he called his "two sets of three"—simple directives for good behavior: His first set dealt with integrity:

1. Never lie.
2. Never cheat.
3. Never steal.

Dad's second set of three was advice on how to behave when things don't work out right:

1. Don't whine.
2. Don't complain.
3. Don't make excuses.

His "two sets of three" were evident in his actions. He was consistent in word and deed, a model of the strength and self-confidence that comes with character.

Joshua Hugh Wooden worked hard to support his family on our farm in Centerton, Indiana, and though cash was in short supply, we always had food on the table. Mom canned fruits and vegetables; Dad butchered hogs and chickens. Even in the darkest days of winter we might have pork chops, carrots, fresh milk, and cherry cobbler for supper.

When bad fortune forced us off the farm in 1926, we moved into nearby Martinsville, where my father found work at a local sanitarium.

My dad believed that people should have a worthwhile and productive philosophy of life if they are to amount to anything. Although I fall short in living up to his teachings, I have found them to be meaningful in every phase of life—especially when it comes to leadership.

Let me share the primary concepts that stuck with me when I went out on my own after graduating from Purdue University—ideas that, in turn, led to my own approach to competition and success.

I will also share some basics of leadership from two other men of character who informed my teaching.

Scattered around the farmland where I grew up in Centerton, Indiana, were gravel pits. The county would pay local farmers to take a team of mules or horses into a pit and haul out loads of gravel for use on Morgan County roads. Some pits were deeper than others, and it would be tough for a team to pull a wagon filled with gravel out through the wet sand and up a steep incline.

One steamy summer day a young farmer—20 years old or so—was trying to get his team of horses to pull a fully loaded wagon out of the pit. He was whipping and cursing those two beautiful plow horses that were frothing at the mouth, stomping, and pulling back from him.

Dad watched for a while and then went over and said to the farmer, "Let me take 'em for you." I think the farmer was relieved to hand over the reins.

First Dad started talking to the horses, almost whispering to them, and stroking their noses with a soft touch. Then he walked between them, holding their bridles and bits while he continued talking—very calmly and gently—as they settled down.

Gradually he stepped out in front of them and gave a little whistle to start them moving forward while he guided the reins. Within moments, those two big plow horses pulled the wagon out of the gravel pit as easy as could be. As if they were happy to do it.

No whip, no temper tantrum, no screaming and swearing by Dad. I've never forgotten what I saw him do *and* how he did it.

Over the years I've seen a lot of leaders act like that angry young farmer who lost control and resorted to force and intimidation. Their results were often the same, that is, no results.

So much more can usually be accomplished with Dad's calm, confident, and steady approach. For many of us, however, the temptation, our first instinct, is to act like the farmer—to use force rather than to apply strength in a measured and even gentle manner. Unfortunately, in my early years the former—force—was close in some respects to my own approach as a leader.

When I see this quote by Abraham Lincoln, I think of my dad and that day in the gravel pit: "There is nothing stronger than gentleness." Dad was a very strong man with a gentle touch.

Know the Difference between Strength and Force

The biggest motivator is a pat on the back from someone you respect—although sometimes that "pat" has to be a little lower and harder. This is true with a team of horses; it's true for members of any team.

Dad understood which pat was necessary and when to give it. He understood the difference between force and strength.

Eventually a lot of Dad's approach became part of my own leadership—sometimes being firm, sometimes being flexible, sometimes having the strength to be gentle, and sometimes having the strength to force compliance.

It takes some maturity—the wisdom of learned experience—to get it right, but when you do, you'll see that although force may on occasion be appropriate, there is usually nothing stronger than gentleness.

Leadership Strength

Some observers would laugh at the notion that I was ever gentle in my approach to coaching. In one sense, they might be correct. I had a *very* no-nonsense attitude and could be stern and demanding; many would say "strict." I could also have a gentle approach like Dad's.

I think I eventually handled criticism in this way, with tolerance and understanding rather than anger or lashing out. For example, in 1970 at the team banquet following the close of our season—one that included a sixth national championship—Bill Seibert was one of the players who spoke to the audience that had gathered to celebrate.

His comments included very sharp personal criticism. Among other things, he said that I had a double standard that favored some players and was lacking in my ability to communicate with the team.

Then in front of everyone, including me, Bill said that his years on the UCLA varsity basketball team had been a very unpleasant experience for him.

I was stunned and embarrassed but not angry. Bill and I spoke later, and, in fact, soon afterward I addressed the team and told them of my willingness to listen and work even harder to be fair and communicative.

My response—a productive reaction—was not what I would have been able to do early in my coaching career. I had gradually been able to bring more of Dad's approach into my teaching.

Additionally, my sincere interest in the lives of those under my supervision was similar to what Joshua Wooden might have done. Before practice I'd talk to individual players: "How's Mom?" "Did your sister enjoy her visit here?" "How'd you do in the math test?" Honest communication unrelated to the serious business ahead—our practice.

During practice we practiced extremely hard, but even then I understood which players needed a gentler approach to criticism and instruction. (Let me also assure you this didn't come easily for me. It takes strength inside to be gentle on the outside. I was no softy—not in the slightest—but I gradually was able to trust myself in following Dad's example when it was appropriate.)

Those I taught, all of them, will tell you that our practices were both businesslike and grueling—extremely so. I believe they would also say that I was able to utilize a gentle touch when appropriate and to crack the whip when necessary.

There is great strength in gentleness—perhaps the greatest strength of all. Without it, your leadership begins to resemble the approach of a prison guard standing watch over a chain gang. Turn your back, and they're gone.

10-MINUTE LESSONS ON LIFE

JOHN GASSENSMITH
South Bend Central Bears,
1941–1943

Occasionally, we took a 10-minute break, and he lectured us about life situations. As we sat on the court around him, he might say, "I want you all to remember the following: (1) Don't smoke. It's not good for you. (2) Respect your parents and coaches. (3) Compliment your mother tonight on how good supper is." His concerns for us went beyond basketball. Coach Wooden cared about our lives.

⇥ MY DAD'S SEVEN-POINT CREED ⇤

When I graduated from Centerton Grade School, Dad gave me a little card that he titled "7 Suggestions to Follow." It was his graduation present to me. While he didn't have much money, it wasn't just a financial concern that prompted his gift but something else.

James Russell Lowell wrote a poem that starts like this: "It's not what we give, but what we share/ For the gift without the giver is bare."

Dad wanted to share something from his heart. This is what he wrote on the card, and, when he handed it to me, he gave a little wink of encouragement and said, "Johnny, follow this and you'll do all right":

1. Be true to yourself.

2. Help others.

3. Make each day your masterpiece.

4. Drink deeply from good books, especially the Good Book.

5. Make friendship a fine art.

6. Build a shelter for a rainy day.

7. Pray for guidance, and count and give thanks for your blessings each day.

Those seven suggestions deeply influenced my behavior as the years went by. In fact, soon enough I was not calling them "suggestions." For many decades I have referred to them as "Dad's Seven-Point Creed." All of them are important, but let me expand on one in particular.

Character and Integrity

Shakespeare wrote the following words in *Hamlet*: "This above all else: to thine own self be true." It was the king's consul, Polonius, offering fatherly advice to his own son, Laertes, before he returned to France.

This same advice, worded differently, was the first of the seven suggestions my father gave me: "Be true to yourself."

Those four words, "Be true to yourself," have been a part of my life ever since—more so, of course, as I matured. Along the way I've given much thought to their meaning: Be true to yourself—to what you believe in your heart is right.

Obviously Dad was encouraging me to stay the course when faced with obstacles. Don't be swayed by fashion or fancy. Stick with what you believe in. But he was also talking about something beyond having the courage of your convictions. He wanted my convictions to be sound and decent. Dad wanted me to do the right thing.

But what is right? That's the real question.

A robber may believe it is right to rob; a politician may believe it is right to accept favors for influence; a man may believe the end justifies the means; all tyrants believe they are right. What is right?

This question is one you must ask and answer, especially when you are in a leadership position. What is right? To *what* should you be true?

These questions go to the heart of who you are as a person and leader, to your character and integrity, to how you treat people.

What is right? What is your answer?

Let me pass along Dad's rule for behaving in an ethical manner—doing what is right. It is simple, to the point, and free of hyperbole. For me it has been the touchstone I return to whenever I seek to answer any question involving integrity, ethics, or character. It was the principle I tried to apply in my relationships with those under my supervision. Here is Dad's simple guide for knowing what is right: "Do unto others as you would have them do unto you."

Why Character Counts

When spring arrived each year in Indiana, the warming weather would slowly soften the ice covering a little pond near our farm. While the ice still looked safe and solid, strong enough to walk on, it was very dangerous.

Some called it "rotten ice." Step on it here, and you were fine; step on it there, and it would give way—you'd fall through. The ice was undependable.

A leader who finds it difficult to abide by the Golden Rule is like that Indiana ice in springtime— undependable, untrustworthy. Without trust between a team and leader, there really is no team at all—just a collection of individuals who don't amount to much.

I have found the Golden Rule to be a good place to start when I seek answers on how to treat members of a team. Unfortunately, too often we see leaders who do not abide by the Golden Rule, who have no basis for behavior and decision making other than what will make them more money.

I'm not suggesting that treating people the way *you* wish to be treated means giving them special favors or what they don't deserve. A player who isn't good enough to be a starter, an individual who doesn't have the talent to make the team, won't be a starter and won't be on the team. That's fair. And ultimately the Golden Rule is about fairness and decency—treating people right.

If that rule strikes you as being out of date, impractical, naïve, or corny, I believe you are wrong. I would not want to be on your team or have you on mine.

Conversely, a leader who treats people right will find that the right kind of people are drawn to his or her organization. Why? Because character counts.

⇥ LIVING UP TO JOSHUA'S STANDARD ⇤

I'm asked, "Coach Wooden, have you abided by your father's advice, followed his example, and been true to what he taught?"

I can only say that I've tried hard to conduct myself in a way that would make him proud. Which means, "No, but I've tried." These words explain it:

> I'm not what I ought to be;
> Not what I want to be;
> Not what I am going to be;
> But I'm thankful I am not what I used to be.

And that's the truth. Whatever progress I made along the way is due in large part to Dad and his teachings.

His was the standard of character I sought to emulate and the standard I aspired to as a teacher and leader.

The coach of my grade school basketball team in Centerton, Indiana, Mr. Earl Warriner, was a man of principle. He was also the principal and intuitively understood the *essence* of what a team is all about.

Can you imagine my good fortune in having him teach me something about leadership when I was young?

Here are the two important leadership lessons he shared with me: (1) No individual on the team is more important than the team. (2) Be willing to suffer the consequences of standing up for your beliefs.

One day when I tried to get special treatment—having Mr. Warriner send a teammate back to our farmhouse to fetch my basketball jersey—he wouldn't let me play in the game. I was benched because I tried to use my position as the team's best player to get a teammate to do what I should have done myself.

When I explained that we'd lose without me in the lineup, he said, "Johnny, there are some things more important than winning."

That's the day I learned that the star of the team is the *team* and not some individual, regardless of the individual's talent. Even though I was the best player, I was benched for trying to get special treatment, for taking advantage of my status. And it was from the bench that I watched as our team was beaten. His lesson is one I put to very good use over the years: The star of the team is the team. Coach Warriner was willing to take the consequences of standing up for his principles even if meant losing.

You might think, "Well, it's easy to stand up for what you believe when it's just a little basketball game for grade school youngsters." You'd be wrong, in my opinion, but here's an example of his principled behavior on an issue involving his livelihood.

When Mr. Warriner was the principal at Green Township Grade School in Indiana, he expelled a student who had done something very bad. The boy's father, a member of the school board, immediately came to Mr. Warriner's office and demanded that his son be allowed back into school immediately or, "I'll have your job, Warriner." And he wasn't kidding.

Mr. Warriner stuck to his guns and suffered the consequences rather than go against what he knew was right. A year later the irate father was off the school board, and they rehired my former teacher and coach. Mr. Warriner was a man who had the courage of his convictions, and his convictions were courageous.

His influence on me has been profound. Earl Warriner would not compromise on principle to save his own skin. He would not kneel at the altar of expedience as so many others do. He was a man of fine character.

⇥ NEVER FLINCH AT FAILURE ⇤

I was taught not to fear making a mistake if it was the right kind of mistake. My college coach at Purdue, Ward "Piggy" Lambert, often told us that the team that makes the most mistakes usually wins.

His point? If you're not making some mistakes, you're not doing anything—not trying to make things happen. And to win basketball games, you have to make something happen. Just like anywhere else.

Coach Lambert taught me to act, initiate, and be bold in execution rather than hang back in fear of failure. Mistakes are part of winning—not dumb mistakes or those caused by haste and sloppiness but mistakes made by intelligent and thoughtful individuals attempting to make something happen. There was never criticism for an intelligent mistake.

Later I taught those under my supervision the same: Prepare, plan, practice hard, and then execute without thought of failure. Mistakes may happen in the process, but a leader can't flinch at failure in this context.

Like my father and Mr. Warriner, Ward "Piggy" Lambert was a man who stood up fearlessly for his principles. He did what he felt was right—what was best for the team. The devotion this inspired in those under his supervision was something I've never forgotten. Coach Lambert was a leader who inspired respect, trust, and love in those he taught.

These men of character provided extraordinary examples for me in my formative years. What they said and did resonated, and I attempted to reflect their principles in my own approach to leadership.

Dad, Earl Warriner, and Coach Ward "Piggy" Lambert were inextricably woven into my leadership system during 40 years as a coach.

⇥ THE IMPORTANCE OF PERSPECTIVE ⇤

Perspective is important. When I was attending Martinsville High School in Indiana, Dad gave me a short essay he had come across on the subject of worry:

> There are really only two things to worry about: whether you are a success or whether you are a failure. If you are a success, there is no cause for worry, and if you are a failure—
>
> There are only two things to worry about: whether you have your health or whether you do not have your health. If you are healthy, a healthy person certainly should not worry, and if you do not have your health—
>
> There are only two things to worry about: whether you regain your health and get well or whether you fail to regain your health and pass on. If you regain your health, there is no cause for worry, and if you fail to regain your health and pass on—
>
> There are only two things to worry about: whether you will go to the place where we all hope to go or whether you go to that other place. If you go to the place where we all hope to go, you should not have worried, and if you go to that other place—
>
> You are going to be with all your friends and the people here.
>
> So why worry?
>
> —ANONYMOUS

Even though it's tongue-in-cheek, I've hung on to it over the years. When things seem to be piling up against you, it's worth a glance.

⇥ Why Concern Leads to Results ⇤

"Worry" is fretting about the future. "Concern" is figuring out future solutions. When you are "concerned," you're going to analyze and determine where and how to improve. If you are "worried," you're just fretting that things won't turn out right regardless of what you do—wringing your hands and imagining bad things.

"Concern" leads to results; "worry" results in losing a good night's sleep. I lost very little sleep fretting; I didn't mind losing sleep figuring out solutions.

⇥ Do Your Very Best ⇤

Although I could rarely sleep much right after a game, I slept very well the night before our team played—even before a national championship game. By then I had made sure that my work was essentially complete.

I had identified, addressed, and resolved my *concerns* and saw no need to fret about the future—and didn't. Don't get me wrong. The outcome of the upcoming game mattered; of course it did.

What mattered more, however, was the deep satisfaction that came over me when I'd given my best effort to prepare—teach—our players how to perform at their highest level and had given them the tools necessary to reach competitive greatness.

You may not believe me, but this is absolutely true: Knowing I had done all I could do as a teacher, coach, and leader provided me greater fulfillment—peace of mind—than outscoring an opponent. (Of course, when both occurred together, it made me feel particularly good.)

Subsequently, I slept well, comfortable in the knowledge that I had done the best of which I was capable. This knowledge is a very soft pillow on which to sleep.

The next time you wake in the middle of the night, ask yourself, "Am I fretting about the future or figuring out what to do?"

If it's the former, have a warm glass of milk and try to get back to sleep. If it's the latter, have a cup of coffee and make some notes.

⫸ Be Careful about Giving Advice ⫷

Joshua Wooden did not pontificate. He was intelligent, well read, and articulate, but he was not one to hold forth. When possible, he preferred *not* to give advice but instead to offer an opinion. It's the difference between telling somebody what to do and offering a suggestion—the difference between acting as if you know it all and acknowledging the possibility that others too have valid opinions and ideas.

Your *opinion*, if you are respected, will often carry more weight than your advice—that is, *telling* somebody what to do.

Most people don't like to be told what to do. Sometimes it's necessary, of course, but often not. As a leader, you must know the difference—when to offer an opinion; when to give advice.

You must also be the kind of individual whose opinion means something.

⇥ Be Generous in Judging Others ⇤

I never—not once—heard my father say an unkind word about another person. This is hard to do, but he accomplished it. Joshua Wooden believed that saying bad things about others is a bad habit.

For all the shortcomings I see in others, I keep in mind that my own failings are many. Tempting as it is to count up and call out when others stumble and fall in their behavior—to shake my head and wag a finger—I attempt to follow Dad's example.

⇥ Luck: the "Residue of Design" ⇤

Luck is part of life, of course, yet leaders who create consistently strong teams seem to enjoy much more good luck than their less productive adversaries. Why is this?

The late Branch Rickey, one of baseball's fine executives, summed it up with great eloquence: "Luck is the residue of design."

Keep in mind, however, that "design"—careful planning and preparation—is not intended to improve luck but rather to remove it from your performance equation.

TOTAL PREPARATION

EDDIE POWELL
South Bend Central
High School Varsity
assistant coach,
Indiana State Teachers
College and UCLA

Coach Wooden left nothing to chance. He had his three-by-five cards, detailing every minute of our practices, even back at South Bend Central, then Indiana State, then UCLA. It was very organized, extremely thorough. He didn't want to leave it up to luck. He wanted to take luck out of it through preparation.

I welcome good luck just as anyone does, but I worked extremely hard to avoid being in a situation in which luck was necessary to produce a favorable outcome or where the luck of an adversary could defeat us.

To me, the residue of design—luck—can be important. Much more important, of course, is design.

⇥ NEVER EMBARRASS A ↤ MEMBER OF THE TEAM

As a young basketball player, I was like most others—a commendation, a compliment, or a pat on the back from my coach was the greatest motivator. Public censure, punishment, or embarrassment, for me, was not.

My grade school coach knew how to discipline without damage. Coach Earl Warriner wouldn't make a fuss about it. If I did something out of line, he simply didn't write my name into the starting lineup. Quietly and without fuss, I was benched.

My high school coach, Glenn Curtis, could be much more heavy-handed. One time he demanded that I apologize to another player in front of the whole team for something that wasn't entirely my fault: specifically, getting into a fight after I had been tripped.

I became so angry at being singled out and publicly rebuked that I ripped off my uniform, took off my sneakers and socks, and threw them on the gym floor. Then I stormed out of practice.

Coach Curtis had embarrassed and antagonized me in front of my teammates. It was unnecessary and unproductive. I was off the team for two weeks.

My college coach, "Piggy" Lambert, was superb in working with those under his supervision. He had an acute understanding of human nature and was the primary model for my own approach to coaching (although it took many years to fully incorporate his skills).

Coach Lambert was a tough disciplinarian. He could be stern, but he never stooped to letting it get personal, never embarrassed or humiliated those he coached. Tough, but fair. Those were his watchwords. I tried to make them mine.

⇥ Welcome Adversity ⇤

My brothers, Danny, Bill, and Maurice, and I all worked our way through college—no scholarships or free ride.

Would I have been happy to have gotten a scholarship? Of course. Did having to do it on my own make me stronger? I think so.

No one welcomes adversity even though we recognize that facing it down makes us stronger. I am convinced that I got more out of going to college because I had to work my way through it than I would have if I had been given a free ride.

Adversity makes you tougher, more capable of dealing with trouble the next time it comes looking for you. Over and over I've seen the great benefit that comes to those who face adversity. Tough times make you tougher. A free ride isn't free.

⇥ Control Your Emotions ⇤

In my early years as a young coach, I was impetuous—a failing in the area of self-control and emotional discipline.

In those days I had many rules that I expected to be obeyed quickly and without question. When they weren't, my reaction could be intemperate.

Gradually, I taught myself not to respond out of anger. I learned to not take events personally but to look at them in a reasoned and productive manner; to work with people, and to study and understand them. I never perfected it, of course, but I tried to keep improving.

In analyzing others, I also looked at myself and saw in my own reactions the trouble that emotionalism could cause.

With effort I became better and better at disciplining my feelings. This became a significant asset in part because I was soon teaching it to players—instructing them that emotional control is as important as knowing how to shoot a free throw.

If you can't control your emotions, your emotions will control you. And when emotions are running the show, you will lose.

⊰ Place the Greatest ⊱ Value on Intensity

I distrust emotion and fear emotionalism. The former leads easily to the latter—out-of-control feelings that diminish your effectiveness.

An emotional leader is apt to lose clear thinking. When this occurs, you are helping the competition—making its job easier.

Emotionalism can be a fatal flaw. I place the greatest value on intensity. It's the difference between a welder's arc and a forest fire. Both have plenty of heat, but the welder's torch cuts through steel with precision, while the forest fire rages out of control and destroys the forest.

Fired up and filled with all kinds of emotion, I've seen many leaders do the same to themselves and their teams. They rant and rave and charge about like a bull in a china shop. Something usually gets broken.

EMOTIONS CAN MAKE YOU VULNERABLE

**KAREEM ABDUL-JABBAR
(LEWIS ALCINDOR, JR.)**
UCLA Varsity, 1967–1969
three national championships

His approach was *very* dispassionate. He taught that big emotions were an extra burden that we didn't need to contend with. Coach Wooden felt that if you needed all kinds of emotion to do your job, then you were vulnerable. There was never any "You gotta go out and kill these guys" talk from Coach Wooden to get us keyed up. He'd say, "I want you to go out there and do your best the way we practiced it." There was never any speech telling us to go out and "win this game!" to get us charged up, no [emotional] juice he tried to put in the mix. We understood that if we played up to the standard he had set in practice, we'd probably win. If not, if we lost, he took the blame and tried to fix it the next practice. He was very focused, very intense. Always, always with his emotions under control.

Emotional volatility is not conducive to consistency and solid performance. I prize consistency, but first I prize *intensity* because it leads to consistency.

Consistency Marks a Champion

The peak that emotionalism creates is followed inevitably by a valley. I do not like peaks and valleys in effort or execution. Ups and downs are not the mark of individuals or teams that achieve competitive greatness.

All else being equal, the individual or team with consistently applied effort and concentration—ongoing intensity—will defeat the emotional and inconsistent opponent.

I worked hard to control emotions as I matured professionally, and I am proud of the fact that only twice in 40 years did I injure our team by being assessed a technical foul. And one of them was a mistake by the referee.

Act the Same, Win or Lose

While it was not true in the beginning, gradually I took control of my emotions. For example, I would not jump up and down after a victory—even if it was for a national title. Nor did I mope when we lost, and we lost some very big games in the last seconds, including a double overtime to North Carolina State in the semifinals of March Madness in 1974.

Win or lose, I tried to behave the same regardless of the outcome. I got that from my dad, who taught me to be wary of those peaks and valleys, to control emotion and not to get so high or low that good judgment would fly out the window.

Nobody could see Dad, but he was there right next to me on the bench. In my early years I perhaps made him wince a few times. Later on I believe he would have been comfortable with my behavior as a leader who was able to control his emotions.

⚜ "Sell" Values and Principles ⚜

A good leader is a good salesperson. First and foremost, we sell ideas to those under our supervision—the team, organization, or group. At their best, these ideas constitute our philosophy—that is, the principles we believe in and strive for; what we do and why we do it; who we are individually and as a team.

What are you selling? What is your philosophy? What is success?

Many leaders stand up and sell "profit," or "quota," or "winning." "Profit," "quota," and "winning" are neither a philosophy nor success but rather what *may* be produced as a by-product, aftereffect, or consequence.

As my leadership matured, I stopped selling "winning"—avoided even saying the word—and began selling a set of principles and values that are the prerequisites for achieving *success* as I came to define it. These qualities are embodied in the Pyramid of Success.

Why any of this was even necessary goes back to my first days as an English teacher and coach at Dayton High School in Kentucky.

⚔ The Wrong Standard of Success ⚔

In the classroom I quickly became very uncomfortable—even distraught—with the standards many parents were imposing (unfairly, in my opinion) on their children, demanding top grades regardless of the youngster's raw ability, sincere effort, and good attendance.

On the basketball court, I would see an irate father belittle his son for not making the starting lineup. "What's *wrong* with the boy?" I would be asked. I had no answer.

The boy was doing just fine, the best he could and yet was derided for it. There was nothing wrong with the boy; there was something wrong with the boy's father and his standard of success.

These things and more had a profoundly disturbing impact on me. Thus, within months of graduating from Purdue University, I became a student again—seeking answers, searching for a better grading system on what it means to succeed.

⚔ Troubling Questions ⚔

Things haven't changed much. When I was young, *success* meant the same to most people that it does now: fame, fortune, power. In the classroom it meant top grades; in coaching, winning games; in business, big profit; in politics, power.

Do your best and lose? You're a loser. Face a second-rate competitor or get lucky and win without giving your best? You're a winner. Both these standards are, in my opinion, wrong. Should I feel like a failure after having done my best? No. Should I feel like a winner when I fail to deliver my total effort and ability? No.

But in my coaching and teaching at Dayton, I saw these attitudes every day, and it drove me to seek a better approach—a more productive definition and standard of success, both for my students and for myself. The search led me back to my roots.

⇥ THE GIFT OF SUCCESS ⇤

A good father gives certain gifts to his children that can't be opened for many years. When Joshua Wooden first gave me the gift of his philosophy of success, I couldn't fully appreciate the wisdom in his words. I was too young.

As we walked across the hard stubble in the fields after the harvest or sat around our wood-burning stove on a chilly night, Dad would say, "Johnny, remember this and remember it well: Never try to be better than somebody else, but never cease trying to be the best *you* can be. You have control over that. Not the other."

That's how he taught me to judge my success—on the quality of my *effort* rather than how I stacked up in comparison to somebody else in basketball, the classroom, or life.

Obviously, we play hard to win regardless of the context, but for me the first and highest priority is making the total effort—100 percent—to become the best I am capable of becoming.

That was my dad's great gift and the starting point for my entire approach to leadership, namely, that success should ultimately be measured by our ceaseless effort to reach our own personal best.

This became the basis for my own definition of success, which I wrote down late one winter night in 1934 in response to the troubling issues I've described when I began teaching and coaching:

"Success is peace of mind which is a direct result of self-satisfaction in knowing you made the *effort* to become the best you are capable of becoming."

As you can see, it's based on what I learned as a young farm boy growing up in Indiana: Do your best. That is success.

⇥ My Success Model ⇤

You can't call yourself a "teacher" if those under your supervision don't learn.

Thus, in 1934 when I coined my definition of *success*, I also understood it was incumbent on me to show those under my supervision *how* to do it. What behavior, attitudes, values, and qualities were necessary to achieve success?

For many subsequent years I sought to answer that question. Early on I chose the structure of a pyramid as the format with which to illustrate the qualities necessary for success as I defined it. Nevertheless, it was a slow deliberative process.

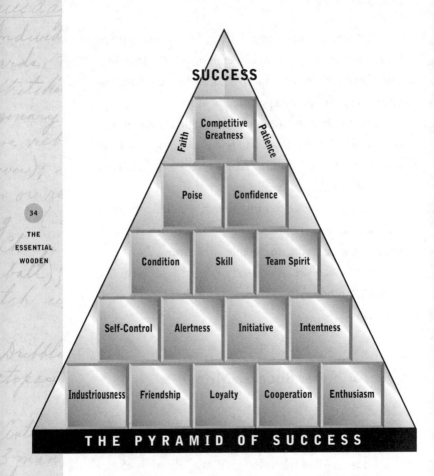

Success is peace of mind which is a direct result
of self-satisfaction in knowing you made the effort
to become the best you are capable of becoming.

Finally, in 1948 I settled on 15 blocks—personal characteristics—and their positions in the Pyramid of Success. Coincidentally, perhaps, I soon was on my way to California as varsity coach of UCLA's basketball team.

The first thing that I pinned up on the wall of my office—Kerckhoff Hall, 301—was a big hand-drawn illustration of my Pyramid of Success.

When interested individuals ask me, then and now, what my leadership is all about at its core, I reply, "My *definition* of success and the Pyramid that defines how to achieve it encompass everything I do as a coach, teacher, and leader."

No aspect of what I taught at UCLA, no element of my leadership, isn't contained in some block of its structure. For me it is the most productive standard and guide for bringing out the best in those under my supervision and for bringing out the best in myself.

⇥ ETHOS: STANDARDS AND IDEALS ⇤

A leader shapes—even sets—the fundamental values and ideals, attitudes, and behavior that flow through and then define an organization. While ingrained primarily by example—yours—I believe it is beneficial to have these characteristics written on the printed page in a form that makes sense. Mine are displayed and described by the individual blocks of the Pyramid of Success.

I chose a pyramid form not only because it symbolizes a structure that stands the test of time but also

INSIDE
KNOWLEDGE

EDDIE EHLERS
South Bend Central Varsity
1939–1941

C oach Wooden can make X's and O's with the best of them, but his leadership was about knowing what is inside you and revealing what is inside him. He had such integrity and sincerity that I would have run through a brick wall for him if he asked.

because it is an effective teaching tool. It has allowed me to share my choices and the logic behind their placement in the structure: a foundation with important cornerstones, tiers that are set atop one another in a particular order, a heart, and an apex.

All these elements are incorporated in my Pyramid of Success. I began by selecting the cornerstones of the foundation.

The Foundation: Industriousness and Enthusiasm

Leaders who reap the bounty of success share most of all a hearty appetite for work, an eagerness to roll up their sleeves and do the job. In all my years I've never seen an exception to this. There will be no harvest without hard work: *Industriousness.*

I chose Industriousness quickly when I began searching for answers. It became the first of the two fundamentals—cornerstones—in the foundation of my Pyramid of Success.

I called this cornerstone "Industriousness" for a reason—namely, the word *work* has been diluted in meaning, leached of substance. What many call *work* is not an acceptable definition or standard to me.

Industriousness is meant to remind us there is no trick, no easy way, no alternative, to old-fashioned work.

It is not possible to achieve success as I define it without Industriousness as a cornerstone of your leadership.

Grind and go through the motions, grin and bear it, work, work, work. But without Enthusiasm, how is it possible to realize your own full competency in bringing out the potential of the organization? How is it possible to build a team that matters? Simply put, you must *like* what you do; your heart must be in it: *Enthusiasm.*

It is the personal quality that transforms work to the high level I seek—Industriousness.

Is it possible to perform at your best with anything but a whole-hearted effort? Of course not. Enthusiasm must be present, or success will be absent.

Enthusiasm comes from the Greek word *entheos,* which means "the god within." Indeed, your Enthusiasm has an almost divine quality in its impact on others. Your energy and spirit stimulate the energy and spirit of team members.

These two cornerstones—Industriousness and Enthusiasm—are the powerful and binding blocks I put in place immediately in the winter of 1934. To me they are self-evident essentials of success—the engine of leadership that is capable of creating a team possessing Competitive Greatness.

Foundation Building Blocks: Friendship, Loyalty, Cooperation

Good leadership requires working effectively with others. Between the two foundation cornerstones—Industriousness and Enthusiasm—I placed three "working-together" building blocks that identify personal qualities necessary for successful leadership.

Friendship brings a spirit of goodwill that nourishes relationships within a group. It takes time and trust to develop, and you may have to work at it, but where it exists, the job of leadership is facilitated and the strength of the team greatly increased.

I don't believe it's necessary or even productive to be "buddies" with those under your supervision, but how can a leader be most effective without a level of mutual respect for and camaraderie with those in the organization?

Friendship between a leader and members of the team, while not always possible, is always preferable. It is facilitated when those under your supervision know they are working *with* you, not for you. Display genuine care and concern for all members of the team.

Loyalty: Do not betray your team, and the team will not betray you. It begins with my father's teaching of the Golden Rule—"Do unto others as you would have them do unto you." Abide by his model and you will find yourself leading a team of individuals who are loyal to you and whose bonds to the organization and its mission are sturdy.

Loyalty is a two-way street. You must give it to receive it. Be fair, be just, and be honest, and you will be a leader who inspires Loyalty and who has the trust of those under your supervision.

It is not possible for an organization to operate at consistently high levels in a competitive environment without Loyalty to a leader who is, in turn, loyal to the team. Loyalty is not bought and sold. You earn it.

Cooperation: "One hand washes the other" is a pretty good explanation of my third block in the "working-together" values.

Cooperation is present within a team when a leader is more concerned with *what's* right than *who's* right and with the best way rather than "my way." It's present in an environment in which no one cares who gets the credit. This approach fosters creativity, which in turn brings about improvement.

Individually, each finger on your hand is weak. Working together—cooperating—they can paint a masterpiece.

A leader's job is to build a team capable of producing a masterpiece. This can happen only when Cooperation is plentiful and everyone is working together.

These five blocks—Industriousness, Enthusiasm, Friendship, Loyalty, and Cooperation—form the foundation of the Pyramid of Success. These are powerful personal attributes essential for both you as leader and those you lead. It is a foundation upon which a structure of significance and productivity can be built.

The Second Tier

Self-Control: Control of your team begins with control of yourself. I prize consistency. Ups and downs—peaks and valleys in effort, performance, and production—are the inevitable results of poor personal discipline, especially in the area of emotions.

Poor emotional control degrades the quality of your thinking, judgment, and behavior. Rash decisions flow from emotionalism.

Consistency at high levels, I believe, is the mark of great leadership. Self-Control contributes to consistency in all areas that matter.

You must be disciplined in your choices, and this is possible only when you have the ability to control yourself. If you can't control yourself, how do you expect to exercise control of the team?

Alertness: To be competitive in any arena of competition, mental quickness and keen awareness are prerequisites.

In basketball, a team that is losing can make adjustments at halftime that will turn things around. But that's possible only if Alertness is part of its arsenal.

Without it the same mistakes continue to be made, the same losing results occur.

Be observant, quick to spot a weakness, see a trend, or capitalize on a strength.

Driven leaders often fall prey to their own tunnel vision, oblivious to what's going on right in front of their nose. Unable to see the obvious, let alone what's up around the corner, their team is suddenly outdone by an organization whose leadership prizes Alertness.

Initiative: Failure to act is often the greatest failure of all. A strong leader understands this and has the courage to act, to risk failure, to stand alone if necessary and make a decision.

When the stakes are high, fear of failure can be even higher. Reflection, study, and consultation are welcome elements in the decision-making process. They mean little, however, if the decision-making process produces no decision. You must have Initiative to make things happen.

When it's time to pull the trigger, you must do it.

Intentness: What good is Industriousness and Enthusiasm if they are applied intermittently, only for the short term? They're no good at all. The completing block of the Pyramid's second tier is *Intentness*—a leader's resolute determination to stay the course no matter how fearsome the course may become.

Perhaps I could have used the word *persistence*, or *tenacity*, or *stick-to-itiveness*, but instead I chose *Intentness*. It suggests a stalwart and long-term application of your will; it implies intensity and *serious* intent.

It is so easy to quit, to turn back, to give in. Never do so. Try again, and again. Try harder, smarter, but try again. This is Intentness—perhaps as essential to Success as any personal characteristic I chose for the Pyramid.

The Third Tier

The heart of my Pyramid of Success is its third tier, consisting of three qualities—blocks—that draw on and expand principles and characteristics already in place.

Condition, the first block, addresses character—mental, moral, and physical character. All three are prerequisites for productive leadership. To attain them, you must exercise good judgment, balance, and moderation in all areas. Should I mention common sense?

Dissipation must be eliminated because it leads to a lessening of physical, mental, and moral vigor. You need not be a goody-two-shoes. People are people, and we all are fallible from time to time. Perfection is impossible, but we must constantly strive for *less imperfection*. Self-control is your ally in this struggle.

If you weaken yourself physically, you have less vitality and strength for sound thinking. You are susceptible to making choices that may be inappropriate and to foolishly compromising your principles and values.

Ability may get you to the top, but it takes character to stay there. Condition is the character block of the Pyramid of Success.

Skill: Complete competence—a thorough knowledge of how to execute your leadership responsibilities—is the starting point for this block at the very heart of the Pyramid. But it is only a starting point.

As a leader, you must be a lifelong learner who constantly seeks knowledge and information that will provide you with better methods of helping your team achieve its full competency, to realize its potential as an organization.

You must know what you're doing and be able to do it. You must seek to be skilled in all areas relevant to your job. Alertness is a vital companion in this process.

A leader who is through learning is through. And so is the team such a leader leads.

Team Spirit: Six plow horses pulling in the same direction represent teamwork. However, this is not good enough—merely pulling in the same direction.

Great organizations have a quality beyond simply moving toward a common goal. I call this quality *Team Spirit*, and I define it as an *eagerness* to sacrifice personal interests and glory for the good and greatness of the team.

It is a selfless devotion to the group's welfare and interests; it means putting "we" ahead of "me," which is a formidable task for most people, including leaders.

In this regard, you set the example for Team Spirit by putting your ego in service and support of the team. Friendship, Loyalty, and Cooperation are your able assistants in this process.

The most important team player is you. Leaders must teach those under their supervision that the team's success is their own personal success.

Selflessness is the leadership key to Team Spirit. When you and your organization are infused with the spirit of sharing—ideas, credit, work, information, and experience—here's what happens: The team is greater than the sum of its members.

The Fourth Tier

You are paid to perform under pressure. A leader must not be thrown off or rattled by events—winning, losing, or whatever precedes or follows them. Leadership requires *Poise*.

Be yourself—no posing or pretense; be comfortable in your own skin; avoid judging yourself in comparison to others; and hold fast to your principles and ideals.

All this comes naturally—a dividend or premium—when you put in place the 12 values and virtues, characteristics, and qualities of the first three tiers in the Pyramid of Success—when they are part and parcel of your leadership philosophy and methodology.

Prepare properly, and you will be given Poise.

Next to Poise, near the apex of the Pyramid, is *Confidence*—the knowledge that you and your organization are ready for the competition in whatever form it takes. There is respect for, but no fear of, the competition.

You are comfortable letting the score take care of itself because you have taken care of your preparation: Industriousness, Friendship, Loyalty, Cooperation, Enthusiasm, Self-Control, Alertness, Initiative, Intentness, Condition, Skill, and Team Spirit.

Confidence and Poise are conjoined in a manner much like Industriousness and Enthusiasm. Each is potent by itself, but when combined, they become an identifying characteristic of exceptional leadership and extraordinary organizations.

When they are in place, you have risen above the rest and can set the crowning block of the Pyramid in place: *Competitive Greatness.*

The Apex

My teaching, coaching, and leadership have always been directed toward a very clear objective: building teams whose members are able to perform at their best when their best is needed, who can deliver when it counts—*Competitive Greatness.*

I believe for any leader to achieve this, he or she must also have the capacity to perform at his or her best when needed. And, as I constantly remind those interested in the subject, "Your best is needed *each* day—especially if you are the leader."

Some years—if the talent was there—teams under my supervision won a national championship; other years they did not. But in all years, my goal was constant: Competitive Greatness.

In my view, whether your team is laden with or lean on talent, your role as leader remains the same: specifically, to get the best out of what you've got.

Competitive Greatness includes a love for the hard battle and teaching those under your supervision the same. It is the competition itself—a worthy opponent—that gives you and your organization the opportunity to find out how good you are, to reach deep inside and perform at your best when it counts.

This is Competitive Greatness. In my book, the score doesn't always reveal whether you achieve it.

For over a decade I evaluated and judged the qualities I felt were essential for achieving Success. When all 15 blocks of the Pyramid were in place, I soon came to see that two additional personal qualities had to be present: *Faith* and *Patience*.

I placed them at the top with Competitive Greatness—as symbolic mortar, you might say—as a reminder of their importance at every single stage of your journey as a leader.

From the very beginning you must have Faith that things will work out as they should—that genuine and intelligently applied effort is rewarded, although not always in the manner you may expect or desire.

Regardless of your talent or the abilities of those under your supervision, you do not control the future no matter how great your effort. However, every block of the Pyramid *can* be under your control. Take control and have Faith in what the future holds.

Similarly, Patience is a partner in the process of building anything worthwhile. Impatience (a characteristic I was plagued with as a young leader) works counter to productivity and progress. It is a hindrance to achieving that which is meaningful, especially Competitive Greatness.

Patience is not just sitting there twiddling your thumbs waiting to see what the future brings. Rather, it is calm self-possession in confronting the necessary fits

TEACHING AND LEARNING

DOUG MCINTOSH
UCLA Varsity, 1964–1966
two national championships

H e gave us printed copies of the *Pyramid of Success*, but he didn't sit us down and lecture us on it. He taught it in what he did. For example, one of the ways he taught Team Spirit was to have us acknowledge the other player who made an assist or made an outstanding play. That's team spirit. He was teaching the Pyramid, and we didn't even realize it until later.

and starts, obstacles and delays that are part and parcel of achieving anything worthwhile.

A farmer who plants crops in the spring understands most of all that good things take time. You must have Patience and Faith all along the way. For a good leader, the harvest will come in its time.

⇥ THE PYRAMID BECOMES MY GUIDE ⇤

In 1934 when I began thinking about the Pyramid and the values, attitudes, and ideals it would embody, my goal was simply to help those under my supervision—

English students and student-athletes—know what was necessary to achieve success as I defined it.

Soon, however, it became clear that I was creating a blueprint for behavior and beliefs that would define *me* as a leader—that would be my own personal guide to success. One of the reasons it took nearly 15 years to complete is that I was very serious about its content. In a sense, I was constructing my own future as a coach and leader.

The Pyramid of Success has been the benchmark of my leadership since it was finalized in 1948—just a few months before I left Indiana State Teachers College and drove my family out west to California—UCLA.

In my subsequent 27 years as varsity coach of the University of California, Los Angeles, I taught the Pyramid of Success to all those under my supervision. I also tried very hard to reflect the Pyramid's powerful 15 personal qualities in my own behavior. I believe a leader's greatest teaching tool is perhaps his or her own example. I wanted mine to be a powerful asset in teaching, leading, and coaching.

⇥ No Changes ⇤

Looking back, I would not change a thing in the Pyramid. It would have been good 100 years ago, and I believe it will be good 100 years from now.

The cornerstones of the foundation—Industriousness and Enthusiasm, working hard and really enjoying what you're doing—are not going to change. They will always be the cornerstones, the anchor blocks, of your success.

Similarly, we must work with others to add strength to what we do as leaders. This is where Friendship, Loyalty, and Cooperation come into the picture. Is that going to change 100 years from now?

If I had my druthers—and I do—I wouldn't change the position of any block in the foundation of the Pyramid or the tiers above it. Competitive Greatness is at the top because it's the end result—the product—of all that comes before in the four supporting tiers.

Poise and Confidence? They precede Competitive Greatness and are produced by proper preparation, which includes Condition, Skill, and Team Spirit. I don't believe that'll change in the future.

Self-Control, Alertness, Initiative, and Intentness—just below the heart of the Pyramid—are supporting characteristics that facilitate Condition, Skill, and Team Spirit.

And, of course, I want Industriousness and Enthusiasm to be the anchoring characteristics on either side of Friendship, Loyalty, and Cooperation.

I spent many years evaluating the Pyramid's blocks of Success and the order in which they should appear. Today, looking back, I believe it was time well spent.

So no, I wouldn't change a thing even if I were paid a lot of money to do it. It has worked just fine for me the way it is. I believe it may do the same for you and your organization.

But, that's not enough. You must know how to implement all of this in your leadership. You must understand proper preparation and training of a team. Let me offer some examples and ideas on how I tried to accomplish this in my own teaching.

THE WAY OF WOODEN

RAFER JOHNSON
UCLA Varsity, 1958–1959
Gold Medal winner,
1960 Olympics, decathlon

A New Scoreboard of Success

I came to UCLA from Kingsburg, California—a very small Swedish community south of Fresno. You could fit our whole town onto the UCLA campus and have room left over.

Initially it was intimidating because I didn't know how I could possibly compete with all these great players on this big-city campus. That changed immediately the first day of basketball practice.

Coach Wooden said all he wanted from us individually was that we try, as athletes and students, to be as good as we could be. "Just concentrate on that," he said. "Don't worry about whether you're doing better than the next guy. Just give me your best."

Regardless of the different capabilities and skills we brought to UCLA basketball, Coach Wooden promised us that his system had a place for men who were inspired—driven—to do their best. That was all I needed to hear. I could do that—give my best.

The most important thing to Coach Wooden was how we presented ourselves—the *effort* we made—on the court. That was first, even before the score.

My subsequent performance in the 1960 Olympics, held in Rome, had a lot to do with Coach's philosophy of concentrating just on being the best I could be. Don't worry about the score, the medal, the prize; don't worry about the other guy; just concentrate on doing your best. It's that simple.

For those two days of 10 decathlon events, I focused 100 percent on the event that was right in front of me—the 100-meter, 400-meter, and 1,500-meter races, the pole vault, high jump, shot put, javelin, and the others.

I didn't think back to an event or forward about another one coming up later. Just what was right there in front of me—do my best.

That's Coach Wooden's way of doing it, namely, don't worry about the competition, don't worry about a gold medal, or *winning* the race. Just focus on *running* the race that's right in front of you.

He did that in his coaching. I basically saw no difference in him whether we won or lost the game. When we lost, I know he must have been disappointed, but he didn't show it. He'd go over what we did well and what we needed to improve.

This was true whether we won or lost. He had pretty much the same face regardless of the final score.

What *could* change that face was when he felt our effort was lacking. That's what mattered most to John Wooden. And, he taught me to think the same way: "Do your best. Just worry about that." That's what he taught. A new definition of success.

I knew I could do that.

PART II

PREPARATION AND TRAINING OF A TEAM

PRESEASON LETTER TO THE TEAM

I am very interested in each of you as an individual, but I must act in what I consider to be in the best interest of the team for either the moment or the future. Your race or religion will have no bearing on my judgment, but your ability and how it works into my philosophy of team play very definitely will. Furthermore, your personal conduct and adherence to standards [the Pyramid of Success] that I make undoubtedly will be taken into consideration, either consciously or subconsciously.

⇥ What Is Your ⇤
Style of Leadership?

I am not writing here to defend or to sell but to explain what I do and why I do things—my approach to an organization's training, preparation, and performance—while recognizing that no system, no one philosophy or method, works for everybody.

Some leaders are out in front carrying a banner; others drive from behind with a whip. Some do both; some neither, like the fellow in Cleveland who tacked this reminder to his bulletin board:

> When in doubt, mumble.
> When in trouble, delegate.
> When in charge, ponder.

My style and system have worked for me, and perhaps there are aspects of them that will benefit you. Or, equally important, you may acquire a greater appreciation of what to avoid. As Abraham Lincoln said, "You can learn something from every person you meet—even if it's what *not* to do." But that's still learning.

⇥ Emphasize a United Effort ⇤

For 40 years I was a varsity coach at the high school or college level. During those four decades my business was basketball. Yours, today, may be manufacturing basketballs—or marketing or distributing or selling them. Or something else.

Regardless, then and now, a primary objective of our leadership is to build a team united and working at its highest and hardest level toward the goal or goals we determine. Achieving this is not as simple as it sounds to some.

For me it began, in part, by teaching—informing—those under my supervision of the following: (1) Unity produces our greatest strength. (2) I am the one who decides how we achieve it.

That message is one I had to repeat, reinforce, and explain in different ways at different times.

⇥ WORK TO BE UNITED ⇤

Preseason Letter to the Team

1965

In every group activity there must be supervision and leadership and a disciplined effort by all, or much of our united strength will be dissipated pulling against ourselves.

If you discipline yourself toward team effort under the supervision of the one in charge, even though you may not always agree with my decisions, much can and will be accomplished. Your lot is certain failure without discipline in this regard.

⇥ KEEP IT PLAIN AND SIMPLE ⇤

Any exposition on leadership can get complicated in translation to the printed page. It behooves us to be succinct and strive for clarity. I will.

My friend, the late Abe Lemons, a fine and funny basketball coach at Oklahoma, liked to tell the story about a track coach in Texas who strove for clarity, who kept things plain and simple.

Just before the race began, he gave his number 1 runner these last minute instructions: "Stay to your left and get back here as soon as you can."

I will attempt to follow the modest model of Abe's friend, the track coach who understood the effectiveness of keeping it plain and simple.

This explains, perhaps, why I am wary when told something is too complicated for the average person— perhaps members of your team—to understand. It's your job to make things understandable.

Albert Einstein was able to keep nuclear fusion plain and simple: $E = MC^2$. Are the fundamentals of your leadership philosophy more complicated than nuclear fusion?

If so, perhaps you're doing something wrong.

⇥ How to Teach ⇤

My classroom was the basketball court. It was there that I taught everything from correct hand and foot movement to values and attitudes, including enthusiasm, loyalty, self-control, and more. (Perhaps correct foot movement isn't on your list of essentials, but certainly enthusiasm is.)

All of it was taught using the same method—the Four Laws of Learning:

1. Explanation
2. Demonstration
3. Imitation (correction when necessary)
4. Repetition

These Four Laws of Learning will work pretty well for improving the performance of any team, organization, or group.

Embrace the Most Powerful Leadership Law

Let me suggest that the Four Laws of Learning may be summarized as follows: teaching by word and teaching by deed.

Of these, the most important is teaching by deed—your example, role model, demonstration. "Do as I *say*, not as I do" is a bad leadership methodology. Words can be powerful, but the power of the individual example—yours—is much greater.

At the start of a season, for example, I would hand out copies of the Pyramid of Success, review it, and have it posted behind my desk in the office.

Players weren't asked to recite or memorize it. The Pyramid was taught primarily through my own behavior and my deeds.

What values, ideals, and attitudes do you want your team to embrace? Industriousness? Promptness? Creativity? Enthusiasm? Open-mindedness? Cooperation? Self-control? Skill? Team spirit? Poise and Confidence? Competitive greatness? And more?

Exhibit them in your own beliefs and behavior, and the organization you lead will do likewise. Not automatically, not immediately, not without various forms of additional persuasion, but those under your supervision will model your behavior in these and other important areas.

Some won't, of course. They will show you by *their* deeds that your organization is not for them. As a responsible leader, you must not hinder them from finding a better fit with another organization. This begins, of course, by removing them from your team.

Be Hardest on Yourself

Make your personal standard of performance—your behavior in all areas—so exemplary that those under your supervision will find it hard to match, harder to surpass.

Be hardest on yourself—the model for what you want your team to become. Don't look for others to be your quality control expert. Be your own harshest critic.

Expect More Than Compliance

Players understood that merely doing what they were expected to do wasn't good enough. I wanted them to push harder, think better, reach higher.

Dave Meyers, a member of our 1975 team, the last I ever coached, expressed it well: "If you arrived at a 3 o'clock meeting at 3 o'clock, you were late." Dave knew that simply complying with the minimum daily requirement was inadequate.

SHOW AND TELL

**KAREEM ABDUL-JABBAR
(LEWIS ALCINDOR, JR.)**
UCLA Varsity, 1967–1969
three national championships

He didn't just *tell* us how something should be done. He showed us. Coach Wooden was right out there on the court with us demonstrating even though he must have been 40 years older than us. This means something—to see him out there doing it himself.

Get Out on "the Floor"

A good coach is out on the floor with the team—demonstrating, instructing, correcting, and rubbing and bumping elbows.

Is the same true in your job? How can you be effective if you're hidden away in your office? How do you build relationships if your team members never see you? Or if they never get the chance to rub elbows with you?

A coach who stays in the office sending out memos to the players won't have much of a team. Leadership requires that you lace up your sneakers and get out on the floor.

WORK HARD
OR LEAVE

DAVE MEYERS
UCLA Varsity
1973–1975

He loved sharpness. If Coach Wooden didn't see it in practice, that intensity of attention and execution—the *effort*—he might say very coldly, "O.K., we're through today. You didn't come here to work." Marques Johnson or one of us would say, "No, no, no. We'll get it going. C'mon, we'll get it going." Almost pleading with him to give us another chance to work harder.

Maybe his Midwestern upbringing, that lifestyle, put a love of hard work into him. Coach Wooden loved hard work. He wanted to see it from the players. If not, no yelling or screaming, he'd just threaten to end practice. And he wasn't afraid to follow through on the threat.

⇥ THE PRACTICE FLOOR ⇤

Preseason Letter to the Team

1968

Although I am very interested in each of you as an individual, when you are on the practice floor, my interest in you is only as part of our team. Your position or situation on our team will depend upon how you perform in comparison with your teammates.

How Hard to Push

I heard this once and it stuck: "They're gonna talk about you if you work 'em too hard, and they're gonna talk about you if you don't work 'em hard enough. Either way, they're gonna talk about you. You might as well work 'em too hard."

This is hyperbole, but there is a valid point made, namely, that the pace of performance—how hard your organization works—is up to you, the leader. Figuring out the most productive pace is the challenging part.

While the two-hour practice at UCLA was demanding, it was not mindlessly so. My intent was to maximize improvement, including conditioning, but not to push so hard that injuries or illness resulted—not to move along so quickly that learning was limited or mistakes of haste inevitable.

The pace of performance by every player on our squad was near total capacity—the team was taut, like a ship under sail at sea. No slack, no sails flapping in the breeze.

A leader must seek to achieve that peak point of performance and execution. I worked extremely hard to accomplish that through precise management of our practices and what preceded them, namely, the planning of the practice.

Our Daily Goal

Pressure is healthy. It can lead to improvement. Stress is unhealthy. It can lead to mistakes.

I wanted our team members to feel pressure so that their opponents would feel stress. I applied this pressure on the practice floor by creating a buzzing businesslike atmosphere that had an intensity and focus equal to an actual game.

I removed stress—the kind that comes from a fear of losing or an overeager appetite to win—by focusing exclusively on improvement and teaching the team that ongoing and maximum progress was the standard, our daily goal. I never mentioned winning or beating an upcoming opponent.

While there might be some incidents of levity during practice—and certainly I don't object to humor if done in an appropriate manner at a suitable moment—I expected nothing short of total effort and concentration in all ways on the practice floor.

Those under my supervision were not there just to loosen up and run through their paces. Not at all. They did that *before* I blew the whistle signifying that class was in session—that the pressure to improve was about to be applied.

⤙ My Key to Organization ⤕

Organization became a primary asset of my coaching methodology—the ability to use time with great efficiency. Practices were taut and fast-moving. I was able to accomplish this with three-by-five cards and the meticulous advance planning that went into what was written on them.

It became very important to me that we start and *stop* on time. Neither is more important than the other. The three-by-five cards I carried kept the train running on a tight, fast schedule. They contained the entire day's practice broken down minute by minute—what we would do from 3:30 to 3:35 and from 3:35 to 3:45, at which time I'd blow the whistle to stop and call out the next sequence, which might be a three-on-one conditioner for seven minutes followed by a different five-minute drill. One after another after another interrupted only for *precise* and *concise* instruction and demonstration.

Each and every aspect of the process—including precisely what everybody was supposed to be doing as well as when and where it would done—was painstakingly etched on each card.

There wasn't one second in the whole practice when anybody was standing around wondering what would come next; no one loafed and looked at others who were working.

Everything had a purpose; everything was done efficiently and quickly. The whole thing was synchronized; each hour offered up 60 minutes, and I squeezed every second out of every minute.

Players felt, at times, that the actual game against an opponent was slower than our practice in the gym. That's exactly the way I designed it.

The assistant coaches and team manager also had three-by-five cards because at the end of a certain drill we might go to another area while we split up the squad, which meant that we needed certain equipment and personnel under each basket.

I would cringe at those increasingly rare moments that were wasted searching for equipment or waiting for someone to get in place. In the last decade of my coaching, those moments were extremely uncommon.

This refined organization of time, which is a skill I developed over the years, was a fundamental key to our productivity as a group.

Without it I wonder if the UCLA basketball team would have won a single national championship under my supervision. Unlikely perhaps. Organization was one of our superstars.

⇥ THE KEY TO GREATNESS ⇤

If you looked at my outline and organization plan for a practice in 1949 and compared it to its counterpart in 1975, you'd wonder how I got anything done in 1949.

Year to year there were changes, little improvements, seemingly inconsequential adjustments, that gradually added up to big changes. (For example, I was careless in the beginning about ending a practice on time. This meant I could be careless about keeping to a schedule during the practice itself because I knew we could slop over. This is bad. Making the commitment to end on time—a small change—forced me to improve the organization and execution of the entire practice. It's not overstating it to say that we may have accomplished more in two hours than some did in four.)

By the time I arrived at UCLA, we started each practice exactly on time and finished exactly on time. In between the start and finish, things ran like a fine-tuned Swiss watch.

Whether you are a coach or a middle manager in a large corporation, I am convinced that a significant difference between your organization and your rival's comes down to details of organization and execution. It's the difference between being competitive and having *competitive greatness*.

⇥ My Expectations of You ⇤
Preseason Letter to the Team
1974

If each of you makes every effort to develop to the best of your ability, follow the proper rules of conduct and activity most conducive to good physical condition, subordinate individual acclaim for the welfare of the team, and permit no personality clashes or differences of opinion with teammates or coaches to interfere with your or a teammate's efforts, it will be a very rewarding year. However, failure to live up to these criteria means failure to some degree.

⇥ 10 TEAM TIPS ⇤

1. Be thinking at all times.

2. If you do your best, never lose your temper, and never be out-fought or out-hustled, you'll have nothing to worry about.

3. Without faith and courage, you are lost.

4. Have respect for, without fear of, every opponent, and confidence without cockiness in regard to yourself.

5. Never be a spectator. Be in the fight at all times.

6. Unselfish team play and team spirit are two of the foremost essentials for our success.

7. We have tough battles ahead. Enjoy the thrill of being in a hard fight.

8. Never stoop to playing dirty—play hard and don't complain.

9. Be sure you acknowledge and give credit to a teammate who hits you with a scoring pass or for any fine play he may make.

10. Be a competitor. When the going gets tough, really get going.

WHY WE HAD PRIDE

JOHN GASSENSMITH
South Bend Central Bears
1941–1943

The word "swagger" may not have been a word back then, but it is today. I take it to mean pride in what you do knowing it is superior to those you compete against. Coach Wooden's teams had "swagger," and we didn't even know it. He taught fundamentals, and we worked on them often even late into the season. That preparation may have been why we had that pride.

Concentrate on
Your Own Product

I focused our team's attention on "us" to the exclusion of everything else. Virtually no mention was made of the upcoming opponent—its style, tendencies, or key players. Nor did I talk about the standings or the consequence of other games being played in our conference.

A joke even circulated that UCLA's team manager would go out into the lobby before a game and buy an official program so our players would know who the opponent was.

I told them, "Be concerned with *your* preparation, not theirs; your execution, not theirs; your effort and desire, not theirs.

Don't worry about them. Let *them* worry about you."

While that may strike you as extreme, I was leery of letting attention drift off our own efforts to perform at our highest level of competency. Knowing we could not reach perfection did not stop me from pursuing it.

Some knowledge of opponents is useful. At what point does worrying about "them" diminish attention on "us"?

I focused on us and our pursuit of perfection—the quality of the product that took the court for the opening tip-off of the competition.

⊰ KNOW WHAT TO ⊱ PREPARE FOR

I am a collector of maxims that offer some particular insight or inspiration. One of the most apt of the hundreds I have quoted and used in leadership is the following: Failing to prepare is preparing to fail.

I would be hard-pressed to think of another that is more fitting when it comes to identifying that which prevents an individual or team from achieving success.

However, let me offer an extension of that little saying that is also relevant: Failing to prepare for *failure* can prevent success.

⊰ Capitalization on Imperfection ⊱

Sports psychologists teach *visualization*—"seeing" your-self succeeding and/or performing some task perfectly. I had a different approach.

A basketball team that has a pretty good night will miss 30 percent of its shots. That's a high rate of failure. Consequently, I instructed our players, "Assume every shot will be missed."

I taught them to expect failure—the missed bas-ket—and to be ready to do what comes next: a tip-in, rebound, fast break, or something else. "Don't just stand around waiting to see if the ball goes in. Assume it *won't*; get ready to respond quickly and correctly." (Of course, I taught them what "quickly and correctly" meant.)

In any context, basketball or business, what happens after a missed opportunity, mistake, or failure is crucial.

Perfection is impossible. Capitalizing on imperfec-tion—mistakes—makes all the difference.

Those I coached didn't need to visualize success. Success would take care of itself if they took care of everything else. This included preparing for failure.

⊰ Teach the Habits of Success ⊱

There is no replacement for sound fundamentals and discipline within an organization. They reinforce you in the toughest circumstances. The importance of little things cannot be overemphasized.

In my profession, fundamentals included such "trivial" issues as insisting on double-tying of shoelaces, seeing that uniforms were properly fitted, and getting players in position to rebound every missed shot.

The perfection of those little things—making a habit of doing them right—usually determines if a job is done well or done poorly. It's true for any organization.

What habits of success—fundamentals—are you teaching your organization?

⇥ My Ode to ⇤ Perfected Details

Some snicker
and say I'm ridiculous,
Because with details
I'm meticulous.
But what do you see
near those who succeed?
Perfected details
are ubiquitous.

—Michael James Cronen

⇥ If Opportunity Knocks ⇤ and You're Not Ready

You must proceed with the knowledge that unforeseen events will occur and the absolute belief that some of those unanticipated occurrences will provide opportunity.

THE DETAILS OF PREPARATION

BOB DUNBAR, SR.
South Bend Central Bears
assistant manager, 1942–1943

Practice was in the YMCA in downtown South Bend. Managers had to be there at 5:30 a.m. Coach Wooden wanted us to inspect each player's locker for clean practice uniforms, four pairs of socks—two sweat socks and two light pairs of socks. Prior to practice we had to paint the bottom of players' feet with a protective solution to protect and toughen their feet and then apply foot powder. After practice vitamins were given to each player. The little things were big to Coach Wooden.

I told players who were nonstarters, "Work hard; prepare properly; some day your chance may come. If opportunity comes and you are not prepared, it *may* not come again."

Doug McIntosh, a nonstarter in 1964, heeded my advice to his, and more important our *team's*, advantage. When opportunity knocked 10 minutes into the 1964 national championship game against Duke University, he was prepared for his chance to show competitive greatness.

UCLA's starting center, Fred Slaughter, got off to a slow start, and I signaled down the bench for Doug, who played the rest of the game and was an important reason UCLA won its first national championship in basketball.

Even though logic would have suggested that Doug McIntosh would have little impact in the championship game—probably not even play in it—he prepared as though he *knew* he would be called on, that his chance would come.

When opportunity came knocking, Doug McIntosh was ready.

⇥ Make Your Eyes ⇤ Good Listeners

Listen with your eyes, not just your ears. An injured player would tell me, "I'm O.K., Coach." His body told the truth, not his words. An associate might tell you, "That's a good idea, boss." His eyes tell the truth, not his words.

Bill Walton, an All-American in college and a Hall of Fame NBA player, would often test me, tell me what I could or couldn't do, what he would or wouldn't do.

I didn't listen to Bill's words. I knew exactly what he would do. To his great credit, he knew exactly what I would do. Bill Walton and I got along because we were good listeners. We used our eyes and ears.

As my vision improved over the years, I could watch individuals, alone or in a group, and usually know how they felt about the practice, the team, or me.

I LEARN
WHO'S THE STAR

ANDRE MCCARTER
UCLA Varsity
1974–1976

As a high school player in South Philly at Overbrook High School, I won every honor you could get: MVP, Player of the Year, High School All-American as a junior and senior, and lots of attention. Colleges were promising me things you couldn't believe.

Then I talked to Coach Wooden on a trip to California. He was strictly no frills. He didn't promise me I'd start or anything like that. He promised me only one thing, specifically, that I'd get a very good education with my athletic scholarship—that and a $20 laundry expense.

If I wanted to be "the star," I knew I had to go someplace else. At UCLA the star was Coach Wooden's team. That was his system. The team was the star.

Is there more relevant information for a coach? Is there more powerful information for a leader? My eyes were very good listeners.

⇥ My Normal Expectations ⇤ of Team Members

1. Always be a gentleman.

2. Always be a team player.

3. Always be on time whenever time is involved.

4. Always be learning.

5. Always be enthusiastic, dependable, and cooperative.

6. Always be earning the right to be proud and confident.

7. Always keep emotions under control without losing fight or aggressiveness.

8. Be spirited, not temperamental.

9. Always work to improve, knowing you can never improve enough.

⇥ Me, Me, Me ⇤

There is more pure athleticism today than there was when I was coaching. This, in turn, has led to a tendency to let great players—and some not so great—become one-man shows.

We see a player make a tough layup and then pound his chest in triumph. What is he saying? "Me, me, me!"

Who passed him the ball? Who set the screen? Who got in position for the rebound if he missed? Who was drifting back down court guarding against a fast break by the other team? It certainly was not the man pounding his chest again and again.

If that player wished to pound someone's chest, he should find the teammate who assisted him on the play and pound on his chest while shouting, "Thank you, thank you, thank you."

⇥ WE, WE, WE ⇤

Back in the 1930s when I was coaching at South Bend Central High School, I began requiring that a player who scored a basket give a nod of acknowledgment—a "thank you"—to his teammate who made the assist: "Let him know you appreciate his help, and maybe he'll do it again. Give him a nod, a thumbs-up, a wink."

Jimmy Powers, one of my top players, asked, "Coach Wooden, won't that take up too much time?" I told him, "Jimmy, I'm not asking you to run over there and give him a big hug. A nod will do."

Members of the team can be taught they're a team and not just a bunch of independent operators. Everyone contributes to the success of everyone else. This is called *cooperation*, and it is a value fundamental to my philosophy of competitive greatness. It is a trademark of a real team.

I accomplished this, in part, by instituting my "thank you" rule. I timed it out. It takes less than one second to say thank you. The rewards last much longer.

⇥ The Selfless Superstar ⇤

Lewis Alcindor (later, Kareem Abdul-Jabbar) believed the team came first. I told him, "Lewis, I can design a system that will make you the greatest scorer in the history of college basketball."

Lewis said, "I wouldn't want that, Coach." (Of course, I knew he would say that, or I wouldn't have brought it up in the first place.)

A great player who is not a team player is not a great player. Lewis Alcindor was a great team player. Why? Because his first priority was the success of the team, even at the expense of his own statistics.

⇥ Teach Lessons in ⇤ Bite-Size Pieces

There's a lot more to coaching than blowing a whistle and more to good leadership than telling people what to do. Often things get complicated and cumbersome.

This happened unknowingly to me in the form of a thick notebook with extensive information on my methodology and philosophy—pages and pages of detailed rules, suggestions, dos and don'ts, specifics of execution such as where the eyes should focus when guarding an opponent, and more.

I gave this "encyclopedia" to players at the start of the season, and I expected it to be studied and understood. This didn't seem unreasonable, since I had done the same.

What I didn't think about was that I'd done it over many years. Now I was asking players to absorb it in a few weeks. They didn't.

That's when I stopped piling everything on at once and began to pass out a little information at a time—handouts, mimeographed sheets, notecard reminders on the bulletin board.

Of course, it was important to present the right information at the correct time. It was equally important, though, to cut it up into bite-size pieces that were easily digested.

Good digestion is conducive to good performance.

⇥ GETTING WHAT YOU DESERVE ⇤
Preseason Letter to the Team
1963

There may be double standards at times, as I most certainly will not treat you all alike in every respect. However, I will attempt to give each individual the treatment that he earns and deserves according to my judgment and in keeping with what I consider to be in the best interest of the team. You must accept this in the proper manner if you are to be a positive contributing member of the team, whether you are one who gets to play a lot or one who gets to play very little.

⇥ PUSH THE RIGHT BUTTONS ⇤

No two people are alike. Most of those under your supervision will respond best to support and encouragement within a positive and disciplined environment.

Some need chastisement or withholding of favor. Although uncommon, others respond best to antagonism and need to get angry. Pressing the right buttons is what good leaders know how to do.

Walt Hazzard, a floor leader and All-American on UCLA's national championship team in 1964, came alive when I would rebuke him in front of the team. "I'll show you, Wooden!" was his attitude.

Sidney Wicks, a two-time All-American and member of three national championship teams, also responded well to hard criticism, but it needed to be given to him privately for good results.

Gail Goodrich, another superb player and key to championships in 1964 and 1965, would almost go into a shell if I was hard on him.

Everybody's got buttons, including you. The smart leader knows where the buttons are on those under his or her supervision. The wise leader also knows where his or her *own* buttons are.

⊰ Focus on the Upside ⊱

I used a little psychology to instill confidence. If a player missed a free throw, I would say, "That's good because it means you're going to hit a higher percentage from here on in. If you miss two, that's great because now your percentages really go up."

If somebody missed five in a row, I had him absolutely convinced he'd make the sixth (although I hoped this wouldn't occur at a crucial point in the game).

What I ignored—intentionally—was the fact that if they *made* five in a row, the percentages indicated they'd miss the sixth. But nobody ever brought that up. I got them to focus on the upside, the positive.

An effective leader looks for the positive perspective and can teach others to do the same. There are usually two sides to every story, an upside and a downside. When appropriate, I wanted our focus to be directed to the upside.

⇥ Do Not Cause Your Own Failure ⇤

Preseason Letter to the Team

1969

Recorded history shows us that the underlying reason for the failure of every civilization or cause has been a breakdown from within, and I deeply believe that most potentially great teams that did not measure up to what seemed possible and logical failed to do so because of friction in one way or another from within. Let us not be victimized in such a manner.

⇥ 100 Percent Membership ⇤

I tried hard to allow no cliques, caste systems, or pecking orders to exist within our team. Terms such as "bench-warmer," "sub," or "second team" were not used in my presence or by assistant coaches. Our team manager was never referred to as a "towel boy" or considered the cleanup person.

All these terms suggest "teams within teams," a hierarchy of position or power. A UCLA player in the starting lineup who called a teammate a "benchwarmer" would be warming the bench himself.

I coached *one* team. If you were allowed to become a member of our team, you became a full member—100 percent. There were no second-class citizens—75 or 50 percent members—on any team I ever coached. At least, that was my serious intention.

It's hard for second-class citizens to do a first-rate job—to take pride in their work or the organization that treats them poorly. This is not their fault. It's your fault.

Everybody is a full member—no less than 100 percent, no more than 100 percent. And that includes the leader.

⇥ ADMONITIONS AND TRUISMS ⇤

1. Do nothing that will bring discredit to the team.

2. Develop great personal pride in all aspects of your job.

3. The player who has done his best has done everything, while the player who has done less than his best is a failure.

4. Competition is perhaps 50 percent fight and 50 percent knowledge.

5. Truly believe that you are better than your opponent in fighting spirit and you will be mighty difficult to defeat.

EVERYBODY WORKS TOGETHER

EDDIE POWELL
South Bend Central
High School Varsity
assistant coach,
Indiana State Teachers
College and UCLA

Obviously, everyone has a job to perform, responsibilities to fulfill. But John Wooden had the idea that if you're in a supervisory position, you don't adopt the posture that you're way up here and everybody else is way down there. Instead, he believed we all work together. Somebody makes decisions, yes, but that doesn't make that person superior. Everybody is working together.

⇥ PICTURE THE POSSIBLE ⇤

Dream big, but not too big. I set attainable goals for those under my supervision—the team. Objectives were high but achievable. Those goals and objectives pertained to the level of our preparation—effort—rather than the outcome—winning games.

For example, I never set winning a national championship as our goal. Rather, I would say to the team before certain seasons, "If you pay keen attention, work

BETTER MORE THAN BEST

DAVE MEYERS
UCLA Varsity, 1973–1975
two national championships

Coach Wooden never limited himself by thinking about what's possible. He focused on the "right now" and was more involved with the *better* than the best. Let's get better, not worried about if it makes us best. His whole deal was about improvement—getting better without talking about winning, or beating another team, or winning a national championship. "Let's keep getting better and better," could have been his motto.

---

extremely hard, and exercise good sense off the court, we may be in *contention* for a championship by the end of the season." That's as close to a big promise or dream as I ever got.

Recently, I was being introduced at a seminar by a team manager at a large corporation: "Two years ago our productivity rating was 84 percent," he announced. "I am delighted to report this year's rating is 100 percent!"

The news was greeted with wild applause and cheering. The team had every right to be proud.

The manager then asked enthusiastically: "Are we going to do even better next year?" The applause fizzled.

"How do we get results better than 100 percent?" the team seemed to be thinking. Well, you don't.

That's one of the reasons my stated goals at UCLA were not attached to the percentages of winning and losing. At the conclusion of a 30–0 season—"perfect"—how do I ask the team to improve on it? The team couldn't improve on the record, but members could always improve on the quality of effort. Absolutely always.

Regardless of the statistics, percentages, or record—30–0 or 0–30—my goal was to step up the quality of our effort, preparation, and execution and to strive to get closer and closer to full competency without worrying about the score.

Perhaps this is not your idea of an inspirational message, but it is fundamental to my philosophy and methodology.

"Effort is the measure of the man" according to one philosopher. For me, it is also the measure of our team.

⇥ CONSIDER THE CONSEQUENCES ⇤

Bill Walton was arrested during an antiwar protest at which he and fellow demonstrators lay down on Wilshire Boulevard and blocked all traffic. If he was against the war, that was his business, but I didn't approve of the way he made his feelings known.

I called him to my office and asked, "Bill, while you were blocking traffic, what would have happened if an ambulance taking a critically injured person to the hospital hadn't been able get there in time? What then?"

He looked at me and said quietly, "I didn't think about that, Coach."

There were a few moments of silence. I said, "Next time think about it. Will you do that for me, Bill? When you exercise *your* rights, will you think about what you're doing to somebody else's rights?"

A few days later he came back to my office with a letter full of signatures that he wanted me to sign. It demanded Richard Nixon's resignation.

I smiled and said, "Bill, it's *your* letter. I'm not going to sign it, but I like this approach better than stopping all the traffic down on Wilshire."

After Mr. Nixon resigned, I kidded him: "Bill, do you see how much more effective it is to write a letter than to block traffic? Mr. Nixon resigned when he got it."

❧ EXECUTION OF FUNDAMENTALS ❧

Preseason Letter to the Team

1966

Accept the fact that neatness, cleanliness, politeness, and good manners are qualities that you should acquire and cultivate just as much as the ability to properly execute the fundamentals of the game of basketball.

❧ THE PERFORMANCE IDEAL ❧

My performance ideal for the team was a gradual continuum of improvement—better and better, not up and down, one day good and the next day not so good.

I did not expect miracles. I sought slow, steady, sure improvement. It does not come all at once, but rather hour by hour, day by day.

Ideally our team would play at its highest level in the last half of the last game of the season. That was my vision, the ideal.

In the ten seasons in which UCLA played for the national championship, that's what happened.

Each day some progress, always moving forward, teaching and learning, better and better, until finally the team performs at its full level of competency when it counts: competitive greatness. And often on those occasions when the talent was there, so was a national title.

But regardless of the level of talent, the vision was the same—steady improvement to reach my goal of realizing the full potential within our team.

⇥ End on a Positive Note ⇤

I believe you should close each day on an optimistic and good note. Never, or rarely, discipline your team or specific individuals at the end of the day. (Occasionally I broke this rule if I wanted them to really get the message on one issue or another. Then I would send them home with a stern or negative close to the day—let it sink in overnight. I didn't do this often, however.)

Never get mad and keep them longer or inflict "punishment." It will leave a bad taste for both you and those under your supervision.

WHERE WE WERE GOING

KEN WASHINGTON
UCLA Varsity, 1964–1966
two national championships

John Wooden was not perfect. But he tried hard to get to perfection. That's what he was trying to teach us—perfection. He knew what perfection was. He knew it was impossible to achieve. But he tried to get us as close to it as we could possibly get. That was the goal.

⇥ Love Is Essential ⇤

Care, concern, and a sincere consideration for those on your team is a mark of a good leader. It is not something that makes you appear vulnerable or suggests softness. On the contrary, it is strength. People don't care how much you know until they know how much you care.

For two hours each day during practice we focused hard on basketball. At other times, however, I made a genuine effort to connect with each player's life—his family, his classes, and his interests.

This was easy because, next to my own flesh and blood, they were closest to me—extended family. Their failures and successes were my failures and successes.

I was their leader, but we were a family, and there was genuine love in my heart. Their welfare beyond basketball mattered to me.

However, my love and concern did not extend to the point of allowing any team member to hurt our group with detrimental behavior. This is no different from a parent who loves a child but will not allow the child to damage or destroy the family.

Love them? Yes. Allow them to hurt our team? No. That's when intelligently applied discipline becomes your ally.

⇥ Suggestions for ⇤
All Team Members

1. Never nag, razz, or criticize a teammate.

2. Never expect favors.

3. Never make excuses.

4. Never be selfish, jealous, envious, or egotistical.

5. Never lose faith or patience.

6. Never waste time.

7. Never loaf, sulk, or boast.

8. Never require repeated criticism for the same mistake.

9. Never have reason to be sorry afterward.

WHAT WE REALLY WANTED

JIM POWERS
South Bend Central Bears,
1941–1943
Indiana State Teachers
College Varsity, 1947–1948

Although he was very strict about enforcing his rules, the worst thing that could happen was to have Coach Wooden take me aside and say, "Jim, I'm so disappointed in you." He just nailed you with those words because you wanted to make him proud. You wanted his respect. Getting disciplined was nothing compared to the feeling that you'd let him down or lost his respect.

⇥ LET YOUR HEART TAKE A LOOK ⇤

Good leadership requires all the resources of the head and heart you can muster. Too much from the head and you forget that all leadership is about people; too much from the heart and you can't make those tough decisions that may hurt some of those people.

Getting the proper mix between the head and the heart is challenging. As Wilfred Peterson, author of *The Art of Living*, advises, "The leader uses his heart as well as his head. After he has considered the facts with his head, he lets his heart take a look too." In my early days of coaching, I didn't observe the second part of his advice.

When I started out, I ruled from the head, saw everything in black and white. A rule was a rule (and I had plenty); break it and suffer the consequences.

Caught smoking just once and you were banished from the team—not for a day or a week but for the whole season.

A few years after I joined the faculty at South Bend Central High School in Indiana, one of our top players was caught smoking a cigarette. When I found out, he was immediately cut from the team.

Discouraged, he dropped out of school; out of school, he lost a college scholarship; without a college education, his life changed permanently.

For what? One cigarette. Why? My bad leadership skills and lack of understanding of human nature. I'm still ashamed of what I did.

Making a mistake is acceptable on occasion. Being unfair, even once, is unforgivable. I had done both with this young man—made a mistake and been unfair. I had exhibited leadership at its worst.

⇥ SHADES OF GRAY ⇤

As my leadership skills evolved—improved—I recognized that alternatives and options were necessary and that I needed to factor in the ramifications of my disciplinary actions.

Good judgment was crucial; a sense of fairness, always important; balance essential, of course. All this was hard to do, perhaps impossible, while I was locked into long lists of rules and regulations with automatic penalties applied to each and every one.

It took time, and it wasn't easy for me to ease up and see some shades of gray between the black and white. Fortunately, I came to recognize that without change I would continue to handcuff and hurt myself and our team.

I certainly didn't become wishy-washy, but I was adept at using discipline in a manner that was productive, that was applied appropriately, and that didn't cause damage.

Logic and feelings—the head and the heart. Getting it right, achieving the proper balance, is one of the most challenging areas of leadership.

⇥ Seven Ways to Make ⇤ Your Criticism Count

1. Get *all* of the facts.
2. Don't *lash* out.
3. Be *specific*.
4. Don't make it *personal*.
5. Do it *privately* to avoid embarrassment.
6. Only the *leader* gives criticism.
7. Once done, it's *done*.

⊰ First, the Compliment ⊱

Nobody likes criticism, but criticism is necessary. It is also necessary to offer criticism in a productive manner that creates improvement.

One technique I used was to offer a positive statement—a compliment—before the criticism. Not false praise, not a phony compliment, but something that was sincere.

For example, if I wanted to be critical of a player's lack of tenacity on defense, I might commend his aggressiveness on offense: "No one's better than you at their end of the court. Let's see you match yourself at our end. Then you'll really have something!"

First the commendation; then the criticism; then improvement.

⊰ First, the Criticism ⊱

However, I would occasionally criticize first. Then I'd offer a "pat on the back" to take the sting out of the criticism. I'd offer verbal support or a nod to let the player know I had confidence in him and his ability to do it the right way.

When the incident was over, the player felt that I believed the mistake was a departure from his usual high level of performance.

And, if anyone was watching, my nod to him allowed the individual to save face. The whole incident would take just a few seconds. The results generally lasted much longer.

Keep this in mind: Regardless of whether you offer a compliment first or last, don't say it unless you mean it. And even then don't say it all the time.

⇥ Do What Is Expected of You ⇤

Preseason Letter to the Team

1965

You must discipline yourself to do what is expected of you for the welfare of the team. The coach has many decisions to make, and you will not agree with all of them, but you must respect and accept them. Without supervision and leadership and a disciplined effort by all, much of our united strength will be dissipated by pulling against ourselves. Let us not be victimized by a breakdown from within.

⇥ Proper Perspective on Praise ⇤

We all like to be given meaningful praise. But you become weaker as your need for praise becomes stronger. Therefore, it is good to remind yourself that most praise is usually uninformed.

Ben Hogan, the legendary golfer, was once hitting golf balls on the practice range. An onlooker said, "Great shot, Mr. Hogan, great shot!"

According to the story, Mr. Hogan turned to the bystander and asked, "How can you know it was a great shot when you don't know what shot I was trying to hit?"

Well, most praise is like that. The onlooker sees only the result without understanding what you know.

Turn a deaf ear to praise and criticism, and you'll hear all you need to hear of both.

⇥ Build Confidence ⇤

My general policy in the huddle was to let the assistant coaches or players decide which man would shoot in a crucial situation. Of course, I knew who should take the shot, but I let them figure it out. Only if they figured it out wrong did I overrule.

Among other things, this was a way to show my confidence in their ability to do the job.

Instilling confidence is usually achieved through many small affirmations and acts of inclusion over time. Look for those opportunities to show your team they have your confidence.

This is why I made sure that our assistant coaches were a big part of the leadership and teaching process. They had a great presence during practice, in meetings, during games, and especially at timeouts. Overall I tried to let them do their jobs without constant interference.

A group freed from fear of having to check on *everything* with the leader has an energy for action that is formidable. It gets things done.

⇥ Creating Trust ⇤

How does a leader create trust? Here's how: Do the things you should do and that those under your leadership have a right to expect from you.

Show confidence in their ability to reach their potential. Help them overcome mistakes by getting to the core reason for errors or misjudgments without seeking to blame, condemn, or punish.

Show those under your supervision that you believe they can succeed. Be fair. Be trusting.

In short, be the kind of leader whose team *you'd* like to be a member of.

⇥ First, Knock 'Em Down ⇤

Each week of practice had a certain pattern in my teaching. Early in the week I'd hop all over team members with criticism. Later, as the game approached, I'd ease up somewhat and be more positive and supportive.

First, I'd knock 'em down; later, I'd build them up. I didn't want them going up against another team right after I'd knocked them down.

⇥ When to Say Nothing ⇤

Immediately after a game in which UCLA had outscored the opponent, I said very little. Players felt good enough without my heaping on the praise.

Immediately after a game in which UCLA had been outscored by the opponent, I said very little. Players felt bad enough without my heaping on the criticism.

When a bit of time had passed, that's when I spooned out a little praise or some criticism.

Generally, I tended to criticize in good times and commend in bad times.

THE STAR TREATMENT

MIKE WARREN
UCLA Varsity, 1966–1968
two national championships

S tandards, rules, principles, and values were important and upheld by Coach Wooden. He knew if he enforced them with the best players, it set a tone for the rest of the team. If the star got away with things, everybody thought they could.

⇥ BE QUICK, BUT DON'T HURRY ⇤

Beware of doing things hastily. A productive leader is busy, and sometimes you'll be so busy that you may skim through a task without appropriate focus. You get careless. The consequences can be severe.

I constantly reminded players, "Be quick, but don't hurry." Speedy execution without carelessness was the goal. My own approach to work was similar.

Do it properly the first time; there may not be a second time. I pinned a card to our bulletin board to remind all of an important question: "If you do not have time to do it right, when will you have time to do it over?"

Detailed Preparation and Training

Coach Wooden always carried a No. 2 yellow pencil. It seemed like the only time he didn't have his No. 2 yellow pencil in his hand was when he was holding a basketball.

He wrote everything down, kept track of all kinds of stuff during practice and games. Coach Wooden was amazing when it came to keeping records of our statistics and then training us to improve on them. I still remember that No. 2 yellow pencil.

I also remember we used to have a showboat on our team, a player who was always yelling for the ball and then once he got it would keep it until he took a shot. Then he'd start yelling for the ball again.

One day, during a five-on-five scrimmage, Coach Wooden decided to teach the showboat a lesson about teamwork. Coach took the four of us aside and said to pass the basketball to our teammate the ball hog. Then we were told to run immediately to the middle of the court, all four of us, sit down, and let the showboat play the other team all by himself.

It was Coach's way of showing this guy that everybody helps everybody or nothing gets done.

After that little lesson in sharing, the showboat started passing more often. It was a great way of teaching a lesson that is hard for some people to learn. And Coach did it many different ways.

His strength was in teaching fundamentals through hard work. Nobody raced to the showers when practice was over. Most of us just sat on the bench in the locker room completely whipped—exhausted. Occasionally, the custodian would even come by and plead with us, "C'mon guys, I want to get home for dinner. Take your showers!" Coach worked us hard.

We used to pray for the game to come because practices were so demanding. But it paid off. In 1939 we were 18–2 overall and favored to win the Indiana State High School tournament. Unfortunately, it wasn't meant to be. Just before the Sectionals began, the flu hit everybody on our team. We didn't stand a chance. The Bears lost to our arch-rivals Mishawaka.

Afterward, Coach Wooden said he was proud of us, how we gave it everything we had, that we could hold our heads high. There was disappointment in our locker room, but I don't believe any player felt like a loser. We had given it our best.

Beyond teaching fundamentals, Coach Wooden was aiming at something else.

When the players got rambunctious, a little out of hand, started acting like teenagers, he'd stop *everything* and say very strongly, "Fellas, I want you to become men, not just beat somebody in basketball." And he really meant it. His teaching went beyond just trying to win.

Before games he told us to do our best, never harbor ill-feelings if we lost, never denigrate our opponent and, if they played well, to congratulate them. And, of course, no profanity.

His morality—that basic decency he has—affected me deeply. He was a gentle man who was a *very* strong coach.

I came away from him with a feeling of wanting to do my best in whatever I took on. We were prepared and trained well. And not just for basketball.

PART III

MAINTAINING THE COMPETITIVE EDGE

PRESEASON LETTER
TO THE TEAM

JULY 26, 1970

Your race or religion will have no bearing on my judgment, but your ability and how it works into my philosophy of team play very definitely will. Furthermore, your personal conduct and adherence to standards that I make undoubtedly will be taken into consideration, either consciously or subconsciously.

⇥ Select Most Carefully ⇤

I don't believe a leader has the power to magically instill character into people who don't have it. By the time they arrive at your doorstep, it's usually too late.

A father would ask, "Coach Wooden, will you be able to teach my son character?" My answer was no.

While I could nourish and test his character, give the young man a chance to show character, I was not able to instill character where it didn't exist.

Your ability to choose solid individuals is important. One bad apple is one more than most barrels can stand.

⇥ The Character Questionnaire ⇤

I sought players who had character, not those who *were* characters. How do you know the difference?

During my years as head coach at UCLA, most of our student-athletes came from Los Angeles County and Southern California—near our campus. I was aware of top players in the area from newspapers or phone calls from their family, friends, or the high school coach.

While newspapers provided statistics—top scorers, for example—they didn't give me information in the area of personal qualities such as character.

So, if I thought a player had potential, I sent his high school coach a questionnaire. I began this practice in the 1950s.

Equally important, I sent a questionnaire to five other coaches whose teams had competed against the student-athlete in question. Obviously, I knew many of these local coaches, and they were willing to assist.

WHAT CAN'T BE TAUGHT

GAIL GOODRICH
UCLA Varsity, 1963–1965
two national championships

John Wooden recruited for character and quickness. They were up right there at the top. Maybe Coach felt those two things couldn't be taught. You had to have them already.

I asked each coach to rank the student-athlete in the following areas on a scale of 1 to 10. Generally the questions were judgment calls and unrelated to statistics. Statistics I could get out of the newspapers. Here's a sampling of the questions and qualities I was interested in:

1. Attitude
2. Hustle
3. Cooperativeness
4. Unselfishness
5. Team player
6. Quickness
7. Aggressiveness
8. Timeliness (being on time when time is involved)
9. Personal habits
10. Getting along with teammates

When I received the rankings back from the coaches, I would then make a composite of each category. This gave me a very clear picture of the player's performance in fundamentally important areas.

I would also check school transcripts to find out about grades, extracurricular activities, attendance, or disciplinary problems.

I wanted to know about their parents—divorced, churchgoing, employed (what sort of job). Was the young man a single child? (This was important because I felt that a single child might not be used to sharing with others. The willingness to share was almost as important to me as the ability to make a basket.)

This character questionnaire was very reliable. I can't recall an instance in which the composite failed to provide me an accurate assessment of the individual's strengths and weaknesses in areas *other* than statistics.

Those other areas are crucial and too often minimized when the statistics are impressive.

⊰ How to Influence the Future ⊱

Preseason Letter to the Team

1972, following the eighth national title

I must caution you that you cannot live in the past. The 1971–1972 season is now history, and we must look toward the future. The past cannot change what is to come. The work that you do each and every day is the only true way to improve and prepare yourself for what is to come. You cannot change the past, and you can influence the future only by what you do today.

⊰ The Will to Win ⊱

How do you spot a true competitor—that unique individual who possesses a special quality called the *will to win*? Easy. The competitor with the will to win also has the will to work.

The will to work is easy to spot because it's visible each and every day. It's right in front of you. A great competitor will never cease working hard to be the best that he or she can be. He or she has the will to work.

⊰ Four Values of Respect ⊱

1. Respect for others
2. Respect for sincerity
3. Respect for loyalty
4. Respect for time

⊰ Recruit the Way the Marines Do It ⊱

My son, Jim, joined the Marines when he was a young man. I was proud of him, but I also noticed the Marines didn't sweeten their sales pitch for Jim or anybody else. Hard work, long hours, tough duty, extreme situations, and more were what they offered. All of this to find "a few good men" who wanted to be part of a great team.

Of course, this is a very sound screening device for attracting the right kind of person—the individual eager to pay the necessary price to become a member of that kind of organization.

DEAD TIRED

**KAREEM ABDUL-JABBAR
(LEWIS ALCINDOR, JR.)**
UCLA Varsity, 1967–1969
three national championships

The intensity of the practice was the same intensity as a game. We did everything at top speed without any break for rest. The first six weeks of practice, I'd come back to the dorm, and I couldn't do my homework. I was too tired. I'd have to take a nap for two or three hours and then get up and do my homework at 1 a.m.

Those who applied for membership, who wanted to be part of the team, were not looking for the easy way. They knew it would be tough going and accepted it, even welcomed it.

Unintentionally, I had been doing something similar in my own recruiting. No sweet talk or big promises. Playing time, trophies, or titles were never, ever mentioned. The one big promise I made to candidates was that if they came to UCLA and paid attention, they'd get a very good education.

Over the years I think my approach screened out many individuals who may have been ill-suited for my system. This saved everybody a lot of time. In its own way, my approach had some resemblance to that of the Marine Corps.

⇥ Seek Those Who Seek Challenge ⇤

I wanted players who welcomed the severe rigors imposed on them in practice. I said, "If you want to get out of practice, just tell me. That's all you have to do. I'll let you out of practice. We don't want you here unless you really want to work. Stay home. If you're not sure you'd like to be here, I *want* you to stay home."

Of course, nobody stayed home. The message I was sending simply alerted them to be prepared for very hard work. And to do it without complaint.

I didn't want to have individuals among us who were reluctant to extend themselves mentally and physically. Rather, I sought those who welcomed the rigors required for competitive greatness.

By and large, my selection process ensured this result.

⇥ The Killer Instinct ⇤

Teams under my supervision were tough under pressure; that is, as a rule they didn't break down, get rattled, or succumb to nerves. Let me offer a possible explanation.

Good conditioning, talent, and a strong grasp of fundamentals by all members of our team were part of it. However, these characteristics are common to many groups, and they still stumble when it counts.

In my opinion, our team's ability to perform consistently near its highest level of competency in tight situations came in large part from my philosophy—that is, my definition—of success.

Of the many things I taught, it was perhaps at the top of my list: "Success is peace of mind, which is a direct result of self-satisfaction in knowing you made the *effort* to become the best that you are capable of becoming."

Every member of our team understood this was my highest grading standard. Not the score, not titles, not winning a championship. Rather, "Be able to hold your head high because you made the effort to do your best."

When those on your team accept this idea—not just accept it but really *believe* it—they are in complete control of their success because the quality of their effort is up to them. It's not up to the opponent, fans, the media, or anybody else. We may not control the outcome, but we can control the input—our effort.

Thus, in a critical situation, fear of losing, the outcome, and the nervousness it produces are minimized. In fact, for me both as a player and a coach, nerves didn't exist. I believe I instilled the same steadiness to a large degree in our players.

A talented and well-trained team embracing my philosophy is fearless and goes into battle fiercely dedicated to giving its total effort. Its members will not break down, get rattled, or succumb because of nerves. These team members will deliver; they will get the job done.

Some call it *killer instinct*. I prefer to call it *competitive greatness*.

⇥ The Downside ⇤
of Talent

At the highest levels of corporate competition as well as sports, you must have real talent on your team to win. All leaders know this. What many don't know is how to win *with* talented personnel.

One of the reasons for this is not immediately evident: the more talented the individual, the more difficult it can be to teach that person how to be a team player.

Look around and you see it in sports—organizations that can't seem to win because the superstar is a team of one rather than one member of a team.

The same is true in business. You're just less likely to read about it in the newspapers.

Finding real talent is tough. Getting that talent to sacrifice for the welfare of your team can be even tougher. For me, the solution was simple. I never forgot that a great player who couldn't make the team great wasn't so great after all.

⇥ Ask the Correct Question ⇤

A team has a certain potential. Nevertheless, simply *being* a team—a group of individuals wearing the same uniform or working at the same company—means little when it comes to realizing its potential.

Here's the question to be asked: "We are many, but are we much?" The role of a leader is to make those "many" become "much."

❧ THE TEAM IS ❧
MY FIRST CONSIDERATION
Letter to the Team
1971

The coach must be far more interested in the overall welfare of the team rather than any single individual player and, therefore, must be as certain as possible in the decisions that must be made in regard to the selection of the players and their proper use. I will be the one who is eventually hurt the most by poor or improper judgment in those respects. Many of you will disagree over various decisions, but you must not permit your disagreement to become cancerous and affect your effort to make the most of your abilities.

❧ DISPLAY QUIET CONFIDENCE ❧

A winning attitude permeates most successful organizations. Arrogance is not a winning attitude; it's a losing attitude because it can so easily set the stage for failure.

Quiet and calm confidence is a productive—winning—attitude. It is the feeling that you are preparing—or have prepared—properly and thoroughly.

Attitude too often is the feeling that you no longer need to prepare and improve. In my opinion, you are already the loser when this occurs.

Team members do not necessarily arrive with quiet confidence; they get it from the one in charge—the leader.

Quiet confidence is contagious. Unfortunately, so is arrogance.

⇥ Stay on Top ⇤

The way an individual accepts success is a pretty good test of who you are—a part of your character. This is true whether you are the leader or a member of the team.

If you're content when you reach a goal—satisfied when you get to the top—you will lose the desire to *continue* to improve; you will believe that past success will occur in the future without even greater effort; you will stop listening and learning.

All this is common and explains why great achievers often achieve greatness only once.

I told those under my supervision: Talent may get you to the top, but it takes character to stay there. One important aspect of character is the ceaseless desire to improve.

⇥ Stay with Those ⇤
Who Share the Ball

Styles change; systems change; leaders change; rules change. People? They don't change. One of the things that hasn't changed in humans is an innate selfishness—putting themselves first.

In sports this shows up with individuals who put personal statistics ahead of team success, who'll take a low percentage shot instead of passing the ball to an open teammate: selfishness.

Those under your supervision must be taught that they will succeed only to the degree to which they help their team succeed. For this to occur, they must be eager to assist others, to share the "ball": information, contacts, experience, credit, and ideas.

Smart leaders understand in both sports and business that a ball hog hurts the team.

Those that pass the ball selflessly are the brand of player that helps a team to win.

⇥ The Leader's To-Do List ⇤

1. Promote sincerity, optimism, and enthusiasm.

2. Stamp out pessimism and negative sarcasm.

3. Recognize the value of a valid commendation.

4. When disagreeing, do not become disagreeable.

5. Make sure each person understands his or her specific role in making the team a success.

⇥ Remember the Sore Foot ⇤

You may not be able to run as fast as somebody else, but that shouldn't prevent you from trying to run as fast as *you* can.

Prior to the race, plan, prepare, and practice to execute at your highest level. And then, even if you're not the fastest runner in the field, try your hardest to run your best race.

Who knows? On race day your opponent may have a sore foot.

⊰ Ignore the Past ⊱

Letter to the Team

1970

It has been almost four months since our basketball season came to a close. It was a very successful season [UCLA had won its sixth national championship in seven years], but it is now history and we must look toward the future.

The past cannot change what is to come. It is what you do today that counts, and I sincerely hope that you are looking forward to an outstanding 1970–1971 season and are eager, not just willing, to make the necessary personal sacrifices to reach that goal. All worthwhile accomplishments require sacrifice and hard work.

⊰ Every Player Counts ⊱

Every role counts; every role player is important. Each team member must take pride in his or her job. The leader is the one who teaches pride, especially to those whose roles may be less prominent.

At UCLA a nonstarter needed to know that his job included helping the starter become a better player. This is not a glamorous job, but neither is the work of a clerk, phone operator, or laborer. Most jobs aren't glamorous. (In my opinion, being a head coach isn't glamorous.)

Role players must understand that their jobs count—that they contribute in a meaningful manner to the success of their team.

I don't believe there are any small jobs or inconsequential roles on an efficient and productive team. There are only those few who *think* their job is small or their role inconsequential. A leader must change the person's thinking—or change the person.

⇥ Four Clues to Winning ⇤

1. Hard work and good luck travel together.

2. The competition *always* deserves respect.

3. Hustle can make up for mistakes; haste creates them.

4. Seek character, not characters.

⇥ The Overlooked Award ⇤

At UCLA we had several awards, including Most Valuable Player, the Bruin Bench Award. Perhaps the award that counted most, however, got little public notice. That reward was my quick personal recognition—acknowledgment—for effort and a job done very well, especially the little jobs and tasks of execution that are so important.

My nods of approval and winks of acknowledgment were not given casually or without cause. Those I allowed to join our team were chosen because they were talented; I expected them to be very good. But when one or more showed something special—rose above being "very good"—in effort or improvement during practice, I let them know with a quick nod or wink.

Those you lead are thirsty for your approval. Don't wait until the end of the quarter to give it. When you see someone on your team doing a great job, let that person know right away. It only takes a second.

This is especially true for those with less visible roles. A nod of approval or note of appreciation can mean as much to them as the MVP award means to your top producer.

⇥ PREPARE UNSELFISHLY ⇤

Preseason Letter to the Team

1964

For maximum team accomplishment, each individual must prepare himself to the best of his ability and then put his talents to work for the team. This must be done unselfishly, without thought of personal glory. When no one worries about who will receive the credit, far more can be accomplished in any group activity.

⇥ PROMOTE SPIRIT OVER TEMPERAMENT ⇤

I like spirited players—young men with energy, hustle, and "fight" who put the team first.

I did not welcome those who were temperamental, whose moods were up and down, or who second-guessed, griped, and groused about everything.

Spirited performers are easy to work with—productive and consistent. Not so their temperamental counterparts.

The same is true for leadership. Spirited leaders are more effective and much more productive than those who are constantly tripping over their own moods.

⇥ GO GET THE BALL! ⇤

I want it this way: "Go get the ball!" That's the attitude I want to see. "Go get the ball!" That's the positive approach.

That's what gets something done on *and* off the court. Don't wait for things to happen. While you're sitting around waiting, somebody else will "go get the ball!"

And then what? Suddenly you're playing catch-up.

⇥ COACH LOMBARDI'S PASSION ⇤

One of the greatest coaches in history and a man for whom I have respect, Vince Lombardi, is viewed by many as having been an emotional leader, often raging at players and officials. His temper became famous, yet he enjoyed consistent success.

I am asked, "Coach Wooden, doesn't this fly in the face of your admonitions about emotionalism—being taken over by passion at the expense of performance?"

I am reluctant to judge anyone from afar, but let me suggest the following: Coach Lombardi rarely lost control. Appearances aside, I believe he knew *exactly* what he was doing and why he was doing it. That's the key—control or lack thereof.

Coach Lombardi may have simply been a very fine actor. (Acting is sometimes overlooked as a leadership tool.) But I don't believe he was a leader who lacked self-control.

Anger, disgust, jubilation, or whatever other emotions you might feel become counterproductive when they lead to a lack of self-control and personal discipline.

⇥ I Will Not Deceive You ⇤

Preseason Letter to the Team

1967

If I do not feel there is a place where you can contribute, I would not want you to waste your time, and if you do not feel that you are a part of the team as a whole, then you should drop out. Although I prefer to go too far with a player rather than not far enough, I will drop you when I feel certain that you are wasting your time.

⇥ The Sound of ⇤
Enthusiasm

Don't judge enthusiasm by how loudly somebody talks. Bill Walton's enthusiasm was bubbling over. On the other hand, if you looked at Lewis Alcindor (Kareem Abdul-Jabbar), you'd think he had no enthusiasm at all. He was quiet, almost stoic.

Kareem was just as enthusiastic as Bill; he just didn't make as much noise. Noise is not necessarily enthusiasm. Sometimes it is; sometimes it isn't.

An effective leader knows the difference.

⇥ Don't Make Activity ⇤
Your Litmus Test

I've had some candidates over the years who were quick as could be—all over the court like water bugs. Seeing someone like that, you might think, "He's the straw that stirs the drink."

However, if you *studied* him, you'd see that nothing was being stirred; nothing was getting done. He would force things, overrun, shoot too quickly, back and forth, here and there. Busy, busy, busy. Lots of activity, but accomplishing nothing.

I value enthusiasm and prize initiative. Both, however, must be directed to a productive end: Accomplish something! Otherwise, it's like a very young child who's just learned how to walk—running around full of energy but going nowhere.

Similarly, those under your leadership can be very active and still do nothing. Do not mistake activity for achievement.

⇥ The Greatness of Second Best ⇤

I have often said that Lewis Alcindor (Kareem Abdul-Jabbar) was the most valuable player I ever coached. By this I mean that because of his height and reach, competitiveness, and mental skills, he forced the opposition to change its game more drastically than anyone else I coached.

I have also said that an injury-free Bill Walton might be the *greatest* center I ever coached—perhaps the greatest in college basketball history, and that includes Bill Russell and Wilt Chamberlain.

By this I mean if you made a composite of skills—passing, free throws, scoring, assists, rebounds, and more—Bill Walton would perhaps not be a clear number 1 in any single category, but he was number 2 in *all* categories. At least, in my opinion.

Being number 2 is greatly discounted in this country. All that matters is being number 1. When you find an individual who is number 2 in the categories that count, you have found someone for your organization with potential for greatness.

⇥ Leadership Is Balance ⇤

Although a good argument could be made for the attributes "experience," "concentration," "skill," and the like, it is possible that the simple personal characteristic of "balance" is the most important for a leader and team.

From a mental point of view, balance means keeping all things in perspective, maintaining self-control, and avoiding excessive highs or lows that occur because of luck or misfortune. Balance means not permitting the things over which you have no control to adversely affect the things over which you do have control, and it means retaining your poise during times of turmoil *and* triumph.

These areas of balance are invaluable in leadership because they enable you to keep winning and losing, ups and downs, in perspective.

If the final score—the bottom line—means everything, if it has become all consuming, then you are heading down a dark path. This type of imbalance is not uncommon with ambitious and competitive individuals in any walk of life.

I personally know of coaches at high levels with superb records who suffered nervous breakdowns trying to match their previous achievements, who were obsessed with one thing and one thing alone: winning. They lost balance in their lives, and then they lost everything.

That philosophy—winning is everything—will ultimately become unproductive, even destructive. Prize and strive for mental and emotional balance in all areas of your life. The better your balance, the better your leadership.

⇥ Do What Is Best ⇤ for Your Team

Letter to the Team

1965

You must discipline yourself to do what is expected of you for the welfare of the team. The coach has many decisions to make, and you will not agree with all of them, but you must respect and accept them. Without supervision and leadership and a disciplined effort by all, much of our united strength will be dissipated pulling against ourselves. Let us not be victimized by a breakdown from within.

⇥ Don't Stifle Initiative ⇤

I don't believe in tying down individuals so rigidly that I might hurt their own initiative in any way.

Initiative is a wonderful thing unless it becomes an excuse for selfishness. Then I don't want initiative, and you have to curb it at that point. But, until then, I want to see it.

Sidney Wicks had great initiative as a player during his sophomore year. Unfortunately, it was directed at figuring out ways for Sidney to keep the ball until he could shoot. His initiative did not involve the rest of our team. That's selfishness.

Sitting on the bench watching players who weren't selfish cured Sidney of this sort of initiative. Soon thereafter he helped UCLA win two national championships and was one of the greatest college players in America.

He had figured out how to use his initiative in ways that were not selfish. Sidney became great when he became selfless.

⇥ Six Rules for Creating ⇤ an Effective Team

1. Consider team spirit and morale.

2. Be alert to spot the good competitors and the poor ones.

3. Be alert for potential troublemakers and get rid of them.

4. Give each individual a fair chance and every opportunity he or she earns.

5. Consider fight, determination, courage, and desire.

6. Look for cooperation and good attitude.

⇥ IGNORE PRAISE ↤
AND CRITICISM

The strength of one's character is, in part, revealed by how you respond to both praise and criticism.

I warned players, "Do not let either praise or criticism affect you. Let it wash off." They would nod in understanding as I continued: "If it changes you—praise or criticism—it means you're vulnerable, weak. Praise or criticism, let it wash off."

As they again nodded in agreement, I added this footnote: "Unless it comes from me—the praise and criticism. Then it better not wash off."

⇥ ACCOUNTABILITY ↤
IS KEY

One of my tasks included teaching members of our team to assume *personal* responsibility for their success. Ultimately, it wasn't up to me. Success or failure was in their hands; it was up to them. This area of responsibility went beyond the basketball court.

I posted this note on the team bulletin board:

There is a choice you have to make,
In everything you do.
So keep in mind that in the end,
The choice you make, makes you.

Perhaps I could have added this final line: "The choice you make also makes our team."

All that we accomplished each day in the gym could be quickly undone by poor decisions off the court. I wanted them to understand that their behavior away from the gym affected their performance *at* the gym and in games.

Good decision making in their lives was necessary when I wasn't around to blow the whistle. Otherwise, varying degrees of failure were certain.

⇥ Trust Begets Trust ⇤

Abraham Lincoln's words are worth remembering: "It is better to trust and occasionally be disappointed than to mistrust and be miserable all the time."

Gather together good people; teach them; train them. And then have courage enough to trust them to do what they're supposed to do.

Trust begets trust. Yours begets theirs. Be brave enough to trust, and it will be returned.

⇥ Let Them Do the Job ⇤

Once a game began, I felt my job as coach and teacher should be virtually complete and that I could go into the

ON OUR OWN

BILL MOORE
South Bend Central
High School,
1942

Coach Wooden limited his coaching to the halftime and pregame practice session. Once the game started, we were on our own. He would seldom criticize our game play without making constructive, workable suggestions on how we could improve.

stands and watch without having to give constant instructions from the bench—micromanaging.

I wanted those under my supervision to assume responsibility for doing their job, and I told them the following: "Don't be looking over at me for help or I'll put somebody in who knows what to do."

Those you lead are there to do a job. Let them.

⇥ CREATE A GOOD ENVIRONMENT ⇤

I did not want to be an ogre, but I did want to create an environment for the team that was the most conducive to progress. Thus, I insisted on punctuality and proper dress and grooming for practice and meetings. For example, I wanted individuals to practice with their shirt-tails tucked in, their socks pulled up—to have a neat, clean appearance.

For me, timeliness, orderliness, courtesy, and other such simple ingredients help establish an atmosphere where improvement is likely.

In the early years when we practiced at the old Men's Gym—a facility that was poorly maintained, dusty, and dirty—my manager and I swept and mopped the basketball court ourselves before each practice. I wanted a clean and safe surface for our players.

The environment you create for your organization determines, in part, whether it succeeds. I went to great lengths to ensure that our workplace would produce the best results.

⇥ Your Source ⇤
of Strength
Preseason Letter to the Team
1927

There is much truth in Kipling's Law of the Jungle, *where he says, "The strength of the pack is the wolf, and the strength of the wolf is the pack." If you discipline yourself toward team effort under the supervision of the coach, even though you may not always agree with my decision, much can and will be accomplished. As someone once said, "You will be amazed at how much can be accomplished if no one cares who gets the credit."*

$2 + 2 = 6$

Seldom do the best players make the best team. I sought the right combination of players—that mixture of individuals who worked best together and created the most productive team.

I tried to put a team together that was greater than the sum of the individual players.

GOOD CHEMISTRY IS KEY

Andre McCarter was not the best guard I ever coached. Nor was Pete Trgovich. However, together they were probably the best defensive *pair* of guards I ever had.

Each increased the effectiveness of the other, and together they greatly increased the performance of the whole team in the 1974–1975 season. They had much influence on our winning the national championship. Andre and Pete had the right chemistry.

Many years earlier Walt Hazzard, Gail Goodrich, Keith Erickson, Jack Hirsch, Fred Slaughter, Kenny Washington, Doug McIntosh, and their teammates— national champions in 1964—were perhaps not the best team I ever coached.

However, when it came to togetherness on the court—spirited cohesion—they were unsurpassed by any group I ever had. Again, they had the right chemistry.

A leader looks for individuals whose abilities, personalities, and attitudes enhance and ignite one another.

If all you're looking at is "Who's the best talent?" you may overlook "What's the best team?"

I value talent, and I was always looking for a great player. But even more I was looking for the player, or combination of players, who could make the team great. That was my goal: a great *team* rather than just a team with some great players.

⇥ Play Tall ⇤

I had a very clear request of those I taught: Give me complete commitment and total effort.

An individual who is willing to deliver those two powerful assets to your team is a prized player whether he's seven foot two or two foot seven.

Many times I reminded those I coached, "I don't care how tall you are. I care how tall you play."

⇥ Strive to Attain It ⇤

There is no such thing as an overachiever. We are all *under*achievers to different degrees. No one has ever achieved anything he or she wasn't capable of.

Whatever you have accomplished, you could have accomplished more. Whatever you have done, you could have done it better.

A leader's job is to teach others how to do more, how to do it better, and how to come closer and closer to 100 percent of their own potential.

We cannot achieve perfection, but we can strive to attain it. That's the idea I had in my head throughout my career.

⇥ My Door Is Open ⇤

Preseason Letter to the Team

1972

Come in and talk to me whenever you feel like it, but please remember that it isn't necessarily lack of communication if we fail to agree on your position or the position of another individual on the team. I am and will always be interested in your problems, but I do feel that everyone should do everything possible to work out their own problems rather than become dependent upon others. I have found prayer most helpful when I am troubled, and I believe that all prayers are heard and answered, even though the answer may be "no."

⇥ My Message on ⇤ Team Unity

No chain is stronger than its weakest link. No team is stronger than its weakest member. We must be "all for one and one for all," with each of us giving his best every second of every game and practice.

The team is first; individual credit is second. We have no place for selfishness, egotism, or envy.

I want a team of fighters afraid of no club; not cocky, not conceited; a team that plays hard, plays fair, and always tries its best.

Others may be faster than you are, larger than you are, and have far more ability than you have—but *no one* should ever be your superior in team spirit, fight, determination, ambition, and character.

Have confidence in your team's ability, and your team will be plenty tough to whip.

⇥ HOLD YOUR HEAD HIGH ⇤

Just before our team took to the court before a game, including the 10 to decide a national championship, these were my final words to the players: "Make sure you can hold your head high after this game." They all knew I wasn't talking about the final score.

I did not say it as a fiery exhortation, but with all the seriousness and sincerity I had in me. It was the most important message our players could take with them into the battle: "Do your best. That is success."

Believing that simple truth gave us tremendous strength. Teaching it gave me tremendous satisfaction.

THE WAY OF WOODEN

KEITH ERICKSON
UCLA Varsity, 1963–1965
two national championships

A Genius for Knowing What Makes You Tick

What made Coach Wooden so effective as a leader was his ability to work with every type of person—different temperaments, personalities, styles, and all the rest. He knew how to get them to do it his way, and this included people who were total opposites.

UCLA's Gail Goodrich and Walt Hazzard were the greatest combination of guards in the history of college basketball; the best twosome ever, in my opinion. But they were totally different guys.

With Gail, Coach would come up and sort of cajole him, put his arm around him and low-key it—offer a quiet suggestion, a little compliment. Then he'd give him a pat on the back and walk away. He knew that Gail wouldn't react to sharp criticism; it would hurt his play.

Coach knew a stronger approach worked with Walt. There was no mincing words. He'd say very firmly, "Walt, if you do that again, you're out of here." And if Walt did it again, he'd hear Coach say, "O.K., that's it. Take a shower." Not with any anger, just very stern.

He was so smart in administering discipline, avoiding backing himself into a corner. So with Walt, he'd say, "If you do that *again*. . . ." He didn't want Walt taking a shower before practice was concluded, so he gave him a chance or two to correct the problem. Walt knew he could get away with a little, but not much.

Coach treated each one of us the way we needed to be treated, the way that worked best for each person. Coach believed or understood that no two of us were alike. His understanding of people and how to work with each player individually was evident in practice every day. With me there was no cajoling. He knew a sharp remark would have a positive effect. And I got 'em.

Always Coach Wooden emphasized playing together as a team, a unit, a single group. That was all important, everything.

Our team in 1964—the one that won a national championship—wasn't buddy-buddy off the court, but on the court you'd think we loved each other because there was such camaraderie and selflessness.

Coach Wooden acted as a scout master, den mother, surrogate parent, a second father, drill sergeant—and a man. He was tough as nails, and yet he showed this great love for his wife and kids—his family. To have a coach who was so tough—strong—who loved his wife so much . . . well, it affected my thinking of him. It really brought out respect. He got this great respect from us. And he gave it back.

We got treated like part of the family. Kenny Washington, whose own family lived on the other side of the country, was invited over to the Woodens for holiday dinners so he wouldn't be alone. And there were others.

John Wooden knew what worked for each one of us. He understood what made us tick.

PART IV

NOTES
TO
MYSELF

PRESEASON LETTER
TO THE TEAM

JULY 27, 1967

My experience in teaching and coaching over many years has naturally caused me to become somewhat opinionated in certain areas, but even most of those who are inexperienced will agree that experience is a great, although sometimes hard, teacher.

Belief: A Must for Any Leader

My opinion is this: I believe that in order to accomplish anything as a leader, you must *really believe* in what you are doing. If you question what you are doing in your own mind, then your team is going to question it and you'll have a pretty rough time.

You must believe in what you're doing and the way you are doing it. When you are in doubt, you'd better think about changing.

Ask for 100 Percent

Several years ago I was part of a panel discussion on leadership with several other coaches. Someone in the audience asked the coach sitting beside me—one of the most famous in NFL history—what he expected of his players.

"I expect them to give me 130 percent. I don't care if it's practice or a game. I want 130 percent," he replied. Then the questioner turned to me: "Coach Wooden, what about you?"

I thought for a moment and answered, "Well, after hearing my fellow coach just now, I'm embarrassed to answer your question. All I've been asking for is 100 percent. Maybe I should raise my standards."

My friend, the NFL coach sitting next to me, barked out, "Next question please." Then he turned and gave me a little wink. We were both right, although we had a different way of asking for total effort and commitment.

WHEN IT IS
O.K. TO LOSE

EDDIE POWERS
South Bend Central
High School Varsity
assistant coach,
Indiana State Teachers
College and UCLA

C oach Wooden was *more* upset if we won but didn't work up to our potential than if we lost playing our best.

Nevertheless, I am leery about hyperbole. I set standards that were high but attainable. I requested 100 percent effort; not 101 percent, 110 percent, or 130 percent. You cannot give more than 100 percent. And that's what I requested.

Making an effort of 100 percent is attainable. It's a reasonable request.

⇥ EFFORT: THE ULTIMATE ⇤
SUCCESS VARIABLE

You hear it said—with sarcasm most often—"Well, he gets an *A* for effort. But that's it."

The message? Great effort is small comfort, a meager consolation prize. Few things are further from what I practice and preach.

Great and total effort, individually and as part of a team, is not a consolation prize or a second-rate kind of success. It is, I believe, the top prize, the highest kind of success. All else, fame and fortune, power and prestige, trophies and titles, as well as outscoring an opponent, are merely by-products of *effort*.

Total effort is a true product and the ultimate measure of your success. Some may disparage effort, especially when it doesn't produce victory.

I do not. I teach that total effort is success.

⇥ Leadership and the Short String ⇤

A coach is not allowed even average results. Fans, owners, alumni, the media, and others always have expectations that run too high and too hot. They keep you on a very short string—or try to.

Thus, coaches are often described in one of three ways: "He's looking for a job," "He'd better start looking for a job," or, "He's a legend!"

The first category, "He's looking for a job," means you just got fired. The second category, "He'd better start looking for a job," means you've had a good season, maybe even won a conference title (although perhaps not by enough points).

The third category, "He's a legend," usually means you're dead.

You'll have to agree, coaches are kept on a very short string. This is true in nearly any leadership position of consequence. It comes with the territory.

⇥ Five Reminders to Myself ⇤

1. Be quick, but don't hurry.

2. No opponent deserves to be feared.

3. Every opponent deserves respect.

4. There is no substitute for hard work and meticulous planning.

5. Valid self-analysis brings improvement.

⇥ Be Perfect Now ⇤

To my way of thinking, perfection is beyond the reach of mortals. However, once you die, it's a different story.

Walk through a graveyard and you'll see nothing but tombstones describing how so-and-so was a *perfect* husband or father, wife or mother, even a perfect coach and leader.

I think to myself, "It's a shame all these folks are gone because unlike me they were all perfect—each one absolutely flawless."

Perhaps there is comfort in the knowledge that after we're gone, we too shall be perfect. But in the meantime, this should not stop us—you and me—from seeking perfection while we're still here; from trying to make each day a masterpiece *before* they chisel our names on the gravestones.

⇥ LEADERS WORK PLENTY ⇤

I enjoyed coaching, but some seasons I enjoyed it more than others. Some seasons I was glad when it ended. Strange as it may seem, that might be a season in which we won a national championship.

Nevertheless, it could be long and full of outside distractions, speculation, and things I had no interest in. So I would be sort of glad when it was over.

At no time, however, was *teaching* basketball tiresome or tedious. For me it brought joy. Perhaps that's why I put enthusiasm in the Pyramid as virtually equal to hard work. I knew from personal experience what love for your job can do.

There's an old saying, "If you love your job, you'll never work a day in your life." I don't agree with it in this sense: You will work plenty even if you love your job, but the hard work will bring you deep satisfaction—fulfillment in doing the work itself.

But make no mistake—you will work. It's a little misleading to suggest that loving what you do will somehow eliminate very hard work.

⇥ LESS SELF MAKES YOU SELFLESS ⇤

A leader who preens publicly is no different from a player who calls attention to himself by pounding his chest after making a basket. What are they both saying? "Me, me, me!"

Listen to a good coach following a win. He praises members of the team as if he hadn't been involved with their success.

He accepts blame (at least publicly) for the mistakes made by those under his leadership. A selfless leader puts the team first. A first-rate team is often the reward.

Don't draw attention to yourself; don't be like the fellow in church who coughs loudly just before he puts a coin in the collection plate.

⇥ Whose Team Is It? ⇤

During my coaching years and ever since, I have made a point of refraining from referring to the UCLA Bruins as "my team" or the individuals on it as "my players." I followed the same policy as varsity coach at Indiana State Teachers College and South Bend Central High School.

When asked, "How did you win that game, Coach?" I would correct the reporter and say, "I *didn't* win the game. The players did. Our team outscored the opponent."

This may be a small issue, but it is important to me because it reflects my idea that a team is "owned" by its members. The UCLA Bruins was not *my* team. It was our team.

I was the head coach—part of a team whose members enjoyed joint ownership.

⇥ The Ultimate Appraisal ⇤

We are judged by what we have achieved. Outsiders will look to the won-loss record (in various forms) to ascertain what you have achieved and whether you deserve to be called a "success."

But ultimately the only person who can truly give a valid appraisal of personal success is the individual himself or herself—you for you; me for me.

I understood clearly that I could be fired if I didn't measure up to someone else's determination of success—almost always based on victories—but I also was strong in the belief that *my* appraisal, *my* definition, mattered most of all.

Your appraisal is the ultimate appraisal. It takes fortitude to believe that your opinion matters most. When your appraisal *is* foremost and is based on the quality of the effort you made to reach your personal level of competency, it is as good as gold.

⇥ The Truth of the Matter ⇤

Much attention is given to UCLA's seven consecutive national championships and its 88-game winning streak. What occurred before that, however, receives much less attention—a national championship in 1964 and another in 1965.

Those two titles were perhaps more difficult to achieve than either the seven consecutive championships or the winning streak.

Conditions—our antiquated practice facility, for example—were such in 1964 and 1965 that even now, looking back, I'm most proud of what our team accomplished. But the outside world usually doesn't know much about what a leader and an organization go through along the way.

It's just one more reason to be very skeptical about what the outside world has to say—its appraisal—when it comes to your success and that of your team.

⇻ THREE OF MY ASSETS ⇺

1. I am meticulous.

2. I am organized and very good at time management.

3. I do not feel pressure, because my dad taught me not to measure myself in comparison to others but rather on the quality of my efforts to improve.

⇻ THREE OF MY LIABILITIES ⇺

1. I've had to work hard at being patient.

2. I've had to work hard on self-control of my emotions.

3. I've had to work hard on seeing shades of gray rather than only black and white.

⇥ THE COURAGE TO BE YOURSELF ⇤

Leadership personalities come in all shapes and sizes. It is a mistake to think you should necessarily model yourself after someone else. Learn from others, yes, but be yourself.

Coach Tom Landry of Dallas was a leader I admired greatly. He had his own style and way of doing things. Former Dallas running back Walt Garrison was asked if he'd ever seen Coach Landry smile. "No," said Walt, "but I was on his team for only nine years."

That was Coach Landry's style. Smiling or not smiling has little to do with success. Have the courage to be yourself; have the intelligence to make yourself as good as you can be.

⇥ ATTITUDE: A TOOL TO LEAD BY ⇤

For a period of years at UCLA I was guilty of worrying over some issues that I could do nothing about. It was a form of self-pity, a wasteful attitude.

For example, I was upset because many desirable student-athletes couldn't get into UCLA because of the university's high academic standards. They'd go elsewhere, sometimes play for teams on our schedule. And outscore us!

I also moaned about the poor condition of our practice floor and facility at the old Men's Gym on campus.

Instead of making the most of what we had, I let these and some other things bother me a lot. What did it accomplish? Absolutely nothing—distraction, irritation, frustration. It certainly didn't *help* my efforts to be an effective coach.

Eventually I overcame it, in part, by looking at the positive side of the situation. High academic standards that kept some good athletes from attending UCLA? Well, I wanted intelligent players on the team, and UCLA's standards helped make that happen.

Rundown training facilities at UCLA's Men's Gym? In all honesty, I'm not sure I ever found an upside to that, but I got better at ignoring it.

Perhaps you can learn from my mistake—how I wasted time feeling sorry for myself because of the work conditions I faced.

The more concerned we become over things we can't control, the less we will do to improve those things we *can* control. Nevertheless, this is easier said than done.

I hope you have more luck putting that into action than I did.

⇥ ADVERSITY ACCOMPANIES ⇤ ACHIEVEMENT

When people tell me they've accomplished something "and it wasn't all that hard," I have trouble believing they accomplished very much.

In my experience, adversity usually accompanies achievement. There is a price to pay. Goals achieved with little effort are seldom worthwhile or long-lasting. Rarely do they give much personal satisfaction.

IT'S WHAT YOU LEARN AFTER YOU KNOW IT ALL THAT COUNTS

BILL WALTON
UCLA Varsity, 1972–1974
two national championships

I stopped listening to Coach Wooden in my senior year, 1974. All the things that made us a great team as sophomores and juniors evaporated like dust in the wind. It was after this depressing meltdown [UCLA's 88-game winning streak was broken, and the team lost in the semifinals of the Final Four, which ended the winning streak of seven consecutive championships] that Coach penned his famous maxim, "It's what you learn after you know it all that counts." This prophetic lesson of life was directed specifically to me. I now have the original sitting as the centerpiece on my desk, personally signed by the master teacher himself. And I can see him this very moment slowly shaking his head with that sad, disappointed look on his face—like a father who's been let down.

The price tag for significant achievement is usually significant adversity. We must be willing to pay the price. Perhaps there is comfort in knowing that most others are not willing to do that—to pay the price for success and competitive greatness.

⟩ CHECKLIST FOR ⟨
COMPETITIVE GREATNESS

Review the following 17 characteristics in the Pyramid of Success. Circle any that are lacking in your own leadership:

1. Industriousness
2. Friendship
3. Loyalty
4. Cooperation
5. Enthusiasm
6. Self-Control
7. Alertness
8. Initiative
9. Intentness
10. Condition
11. Skill
12. Team Spirit
13. Poise
14. Confidence
15. Competitive Greatness
16. Faith
17. Patience

Don't be discouraged if you circled a few of the 17 qualities listed above. I also would have circled some of them in the earlier stages of my own career.

There's nothing wrong with acknowledging our shortcomings as long as we take the next step: improving on and then eliminating the liability.

⇥ 24/7 ⇤

There's a phrase common today in the business world that means you're working or thinking about your job 24 hours a day, 7 days a week: "24/7." In fact, one young go-getter told me he was plugged into his job "24/7/365."

I asked, "How much coffee does it take to do that?"

⇥ Not 24/7 ⇤

My approach was different. During practices, two hours each day from 3:30 p.m. until 5:30 p.m., I expected total and absolute concentration and participation in what I was teaching.

However, once practice was over, basketball was over. I asked our players to forget about it, and I told them I didn't want them working out in the weight room or doing anything related to basketball other than observing good personal habits—everything in moderation.

This made me different from some coaches who wanted players to think about basketball all the time, on the court and off the court—the 24/7 approach.

I didn't want that. I wanted players to concentrate on other things—first of all their studies. But I also felt it important to refresh and recharge oneself, not to be so consumed with basketball that it becomes a chore.

Of course, my own duties required attention before and after practice, but at the end of the workday, I went home and left basketball on the basketball court.

My dear wife, Nellie, said she couldn't tell if I'd had a good day or a bad day at practice. I left it behind at the office.

⇥ Productive ⇤
Pressure

I never pressured our players to win a game. I pressured them to work exceedingly hard to reach their own level of competency, but I never put any pressure on them to beat a particular opponent.

This philosophy was taught to me in large part by my father, who said, "Prepare through hard work; don't worry about whether you're better than someone else; always try to be the best that *you* can be."

This philosophy eliminates pressure except for the pressure you put on yourself to think intelligently and work very hard to improve your skills and performance. If you take that responsibility seriously, as I did, it's more pressure than anyone else can put on you.

That's productive pressure—the kind that will ultimately produce competitive greatness.

⇥ Free Flow of Information ⇤

Walt Hazzard was a key player on our 1964 national championship team. His teammates liked to pass the ball to him and did so without hesitation. Why? Because they knew Walt would pass it back to them without hesitation. He was *unselfish*, even though he had the same urge to hang onto the ball that most players have.

One of the things that made him so valuable was his desire to facilitate the "free flow of information"—the ball.

He received the basketball so often because he shared the basketball so much. I have a strong feeling that teams that have Walt Hazzards in their organizations win a lot more often than those that don't.

⇥ Focus on Today ⇤
Preseason Letter to the Team
1968

The past cannot change what is to come. The work that you do each and every day is the only true way to improve and prepare yourself for what is to come. You cannot change the past, and you can influence the future only by what you do today.

⇥ Eye on the Ball ⇤

You must keep your organization thinking in the present, focused on today rather than lingering in the past or dreaming about the future. Team members must truly comprehend that what they do now, this day, determines what they will achieve tomorrow.

The past is for reference; the future for dreamers; the present moment is where your create success.

⇥ Let It Go ⇤

Leadership produces adversaries. Adversaries can produce animosity, anger, even hatred within you. Allowing these emotions to have a home in your heart is self-destructive.

Don't hold a grudge. It takes up room in your heart; it takes up time in your life; it takes up space in your mind. Let it go. Let others hate and be hurt. Don't do it to yourself.

Remember what Mother Teresa said, "Forgiveness will set you free."

⇥ Five Things a Leader ⇤ Should Keep in Mind

1. Adversity thins the ranks of your competitors.

2. Getting individuals to mesh their goals with team goals is your goal.

3. Worthwhile objectives take time, which requires patience, which requires faith that things will work out as they should.

4. You are imperfect; so is everyone else.

5. Meticulous planning is meaningless without hard work.

⫸ WHEN EVERYTHING ISN'T ENOUGH ⫷

Many years ago, Everett Bennett Williams, owner of the Washington Redskins, hired George Allen as head coach. "George," Mr. Williams told his new coach, "do what it takes to produce a Super Bowl winner for us. I'm giving you an *unlimited* budget."

Two months later, so the story goes, George had exceeded the budget.

The tale is not true, but it illustrates a good point: No matter how much you give some people, it's never enough.

More time? More money? More staff? Some people will take all you've got and tell you it's not enough.

You must decide when enough is enough.

⫸ FINDING THE BEST WAY ⫷
Preseason Letter to the Team
1975

It has been said that a true leader is always interested in finding the best way to accomplish something rather than having his or her own way, and I hope that I come under that category. We must work together if we are to measure up to our potential, and anything less than that means some degree of failure.

⇥ Your Pulpit ⇤

Leadership comes with an automatic pulpit. You are expected to talk, to have the answer, to talk, to find a solution, to talk, to make decisions, to talk some more.

Given the pulpit of leadership, it is tempting to pontificate—to talk all the time.

Perhaps the most important part of your job is to *listen*. And learn. When you're holding forth from behind your pulpit, you're not listening, not observing, not learning, not looking for the best way rather than just insisting on your way.

Don't kid yourself. A pulpit is just a fancy soapbox. Any fool can stand on a soapbox and hold forth. Spend too much time on your little soapbox, and somebody's going to come along and kick it out from under you.

Pay attention; listen; learn. Don't get hooked on your pulpit.

⇥ Ignore the Pundits ⇤

In the years following my retirement from UCLA, subsequent coaches were subjected to unfair criticism and comparisons. Critics looked for ways to prove the new head coach fell short in doing things my way as if "my way" was the only correct way.

One new UCLA head coach—an excellent, top-notch coach—thought it would be a nice gesture to host a reception for the media, an opportunity to get acquainted. Of course, beverages—including mixed drinks—were available. It was perfectly reasonable, and the event was a success.

However, the next day our coach was criticized publicly by a local media person for throwing a cocktail party "when his predecessor, John Wooden, would not even attend a cocktail party."

It was an unfair and damaging comparison, but typical of how others will foist their arbitrary standard on you, especially when you have the visibility that comes with leadership.

It takes strength inside to ignore it, to move ahead without letting it affect you. At times, it can be almost unbearable.

Perhaps it helps to know that this is just the way it is.

⇥ Keep Asking ⇤
the Same Question

I was a poor leader when I started because I had all the answers. Improvement came in direct proportion to my willingness to ask the questions.

Here's the most important question I asked: How can I help our team improve? When I thought of something, I did it. Simple as that.

An effective leader keeps asking that question because there's *always* something more you can do—always room for improvement. Always.

When you've asked yourself that question a hundred times, ask it again: "How can I help our team improve?"

A productive leader always finds a new answer, a better way, a superior solution. But only if you keep asking "How can I help the team improve?"

⇥ PUT OTHERS FIRST ⇤

I have great reverence for Abraham Lincoln and Mother Teresa. They were different in many ways, but each had the ability to put others first.

We know that Mr. Lincoln was a strong and able leader, but we may forget that Mother Teresa also created a large and powerful team, the Missionaries of Charity, who helped the poor in Calcutta and around the world.

One of her leadership skills—and President Lincoln's—is available to us if we try: selflessness. Put others first. It's a powerful leadership asset.

⇥ THE ART OF LEADERSHIP ⇤

Mr. Wilfred Peterson lists a number of important rules in regard to leadership in his book *The Art of Leadership*. Some of them are as follows:

1. The leader has faith in people. He believes in, trusts, and thus draws out the best in them.

2. The leader sees through the eyes of his followers.

3. The leader does not say, "Get going!" Instead he says, "Let's go!" and leads the way.

4. The leader uses his heart as well as his head. After he has considered the facts with his head, he lets his heart take a look too.

5. The leader has a sense of humor. He has a humble spirit and can laugh at himself.

6. The leader is a person of action as well as a person of thought.

I would summarize Mr. Peterson's tips this way: A good leader has humility and humor, initiative and compassion, perspective and common sense, and faith in those he leads.

How many of these characteristics do you possess?

⇥ MY GROWTH CURVE ⇤

Lewis Alcindor (later Kareem Abdul-Jabbar) and Bill Walton are the two most famous players I've coached. Teams they were on won five national championships and had a combined record of 174–6 during the years they played at UCLA (Lewis in 1967, 1968, and 1969; Bill in 1972, 1973, and 1974).

Part of the reason the UCLA Bruins did well during those years was my own maturing as a coach. I got better at working with people and understanding human nature.

Lewis came along first. In 1967 he joined the varsity—a superb team player, selfless and sharing, a consummate competitor. Two years later, along came Bill

Walton. While he shared those same qualities with Lewis, the two of them were complete opposites in many other ways.

Lewis was not an introvert, but he was not outgoing either; Bill was the opposite. Lewis never challenged me on anything; Bill tested me on many things. Lewis was not confrontational; Bill liked to challenge authority.

Early in my career I would have taken Bill's "testing" of my authority personally and reacted poorly. (That's exactly what happened with a football player who challenged me at Dayton High School. When he refused my orders to perform a particular drill, I knocked him down.)

It wouldn't have worked between Bill and me if I hadn't found better leadership skills. Fortunately, he came along when I had improved my understanding of human nature and how to work with people.

It would have been a shame if I hadn't been a good enough leader to work effectively with Bill Walton.

⇥ I Stop Talking about Winning ⇤

My high school coach at Martinsville, Indiana, Glenn Curtis, was an excellent teacher of basketball. He also was a master at revving up his team before we took to the court—exhorting us to "win" and impressing upon us the necessity of victory and *beating* the other team. He even used poetry to get us inspired.

Later, at Purdue University, Coach Ward "Piggy" Lambert also spoke of "winning," although not to any

WINNING IS A BY-PRODUCT OF PREPARATION

MIKE WARREN
UCLA Varsity, 1966–1968

I never heard him mention winning in the context of beating a particular opponent. He would say, "I would like to win every game we play, but that's not realistic, but what is possible is playing the best that we can possibly play. Winning becomes a by-product of how well prepared you are mentally, physically."

---

great extent. He might, on occasion, tell us, "Go out there and win this game!" but it was not his common refrain.

When I began coaching, I followed Coach Lambert's example more or less. While I urged the team to "win," it was not something I did before every single game. Nevertheless, I did use it when I thought it appropriate—"Now go out there and beat these guys!"

But after I'd been teaching for a number of years— maybe three or four years—I came to see this approach as one I didn't want to use at all ever again.

My attitude on this changed gradually. Perhaps it was because I sensed it was in contradiction to my belief that total effort rather than winning—the final score—counted most to me, and I wanted it to count most to those I coached.

Thus, I began exhorting the team to "give it your best out there." That gradually evolved to the following: "When you walk back into this locker room after the game, make sure you can hold your head high."

I wanted the players to understand that winning would take care of itself if they took care of their effort—100 percent or as close to it as they could get.

I doubt if you can find a player I coached over the final 30 years of my career who ever heard me talk about winning or exhorted the team to beat the other team.

Once I made the change, I don't think I ever mentioned "winning" again.

⇥ A Leader's Tool Kit ⇤

1. Keep courtesy and consideration for those you lead foremost in your mind.

2. Laugh with, not at, others.

3. Optimism and enthusiasm are more powerful than sarcasm and cynicism.

4. Seek those moments when you can offer a sincere compliment to those who don't get many compliments.

Overcoming the Fear of Mistakes

Almost always a leader is better off building up someone's confidence than knocking it down.

I told players that .400 hitters in baseball go hitless more than half the time; .300 hitters miss more often than not. A manager would welcome a batter who gets only one hit for every three times at bat. That's a .333 batting average!

I wanted our players to understand that I wasn't perfect and neither were they. Mistakes are part of high performance. Don't fear making a mistake if you've prepared properly.

Mind Control

I kept negative thoughts out. But I also kept positive thoughts, such as winning a championship, at bay.

I understood in certain years that a national championship was a possibility, but I didn't dwell on it. What consumed me was teaching players what they needed to know to reach their level of competency, which might put them in a position to win a championship.

In turn, I wanted them consumed with making the effort to learn what I was teaching. Teaching and learning occupied our attention, not whether we might, or might not, win a trophy.

We never took our eye off the basketball and started gazing into the crystal ball called the future.

⇥ The Key Difference ⇤

Among experienced coaches, there is little difference in their technical knowledge of the game. However, there is a vast difference in their ability to motivate and teach the game.

I believe this is true for leaders in most organizations. Knowledge is not enough to get desired results. You must have the more elusive ability to teach and motivate. This defines effective leadership.

If you can't teach and you can't motivate, how can you be a leader?

⇥ Three Be's of Leadership ⇤

1. Be slow to criticize and quick to commend.

2. Be more concerned with what you can do for others than with what they can do for you.

3. Be more concerned with getting ahead than with getting even.

⇥ The Benefit of Composure ⇤

My self-control on the bench improved over the years. While I might have barked out something from time to time at a referee through my rolled-up program—"Don't be a homer!" or "Call 'em the same at both ends"—I was very contained most of the time.

DON'T MOPE
OR GLOAT

LYNN SHACKLEFORD
UCLA Varsity, 1967–1969
three national championships

e used to tell us to walk out of the locker room after a game in such a way that nobody could tell if we won or lost. Coach wanted us to control our emotions always.

One of the reasons I valued composure during a game is quite simple: Emotionalism—flailing about and flaring up, screaming and stomping the floor—tells the team that I've lost it.

Where is your team then? When the one in charge, the leader, loses it?

They're lost. Everybody's lost when you lose it.

⤙ DELUSIONS OF LEADERS ⤛

Two of the symptoms of insanity are delusions of grandeur and delusions of persecution. Anyone who has been a leader for any length of time has had one—or both—of these symptoms.

Being afflicted with either of these delusions only means you're normal—that you've experienced the usual violent ups and downs of leadership.

However, when you hang on to the delusion for more than a few days, that's when you've got a problem.

⇥ Leadership Guidelines ⇤

1. Don't have so many rules that your team develops rigor mortis.

2. Never brush over details.

3. Teach respect for all and fear for none.

4. Have one team, not regulars and substitutes. No one feels good being a "substitute."

⇥ Praying ⇤

I never prayed for victory, never asked God to let our team win the national championship, never offered up a prayer that UCLA would set some record or win a particular game.

To my way of thinking, God has more important things on his mind. Whatever level of competency we reach is up to us—only us.

It's like the story of the Englishman who was walking down a cobblestone path when he came upon a small cottage with a beautiful garden next to it.

The Englishman paused in admiration and said to the gardener who was down on his hands and knees pulling weeds, "Sir, what a beautiful garden God has blessed you with." The gardener replied, "You should have seen it when God was taking care of it by himself."

Whatever gifts the Good Lord may have blessed us with, we are the ones who must get down on our hands and knees and do the work. It's up to us to make the garden beautiful.

⊰ A MAN OF FAITH ⊱

My own Christian faith has given me great strength. I believe those of faith—and not just my faith—have something powerful and true they can draw on.

That's why I encouraged those under my supervision to believe in something—a faith that gave them inner strength: "I don't care what religion you choose, but I think it makes you a better person to believe in *something*."

When Lewis Alcindor (Kareem Abdul-Jabbar) became a Muslim, he did so after careful consideration and study. It didn't bother me. He is still a Muslim, and his faith has given him strength over the years just as my Christian faith does for me.

Occasionally, I wonder how those who don't believe in something get by.

⇥ THE BIG BALLOON ⇤

A healthy ego is a leadership asset. Inflated, however, it becomes a leadership liability. Often it's difficult to tell when you make the crossing from healthy self-esteem— ego—to unhealthy egotism and arrogance.

When it occurs, you begin to shut people out. Unwilling to listen, you hold forth. In a room full of creative people, you take up more and more space like a hot-air balloon that gets bigger and bigger.

Eventually there's no space left in the room. Everybody leaves—or wants to.

⇥ INNER CONFIDENCE ⇤

I never had any fear of losing my job—being fired—at any point in my 40 years of coaching. This was true at Dayton High School in Kentucky, South Bend Central High School, Indiana State Teachers College, and the University of California, Los Angeles.

There are a couple of good reasons for this. First, I felt competent both as a coach and as an English teacher. If an administrator or the school board felt otherwise, I believed I could catch on someplace else.

Second, I never acquired a lifestyle that was difficult to pay for. Nor did I get my salary up so high that I might become "unhireable."

Therefore, in one of the most uncertain professions of all, coaching, I was certain of one thing: No athletic director or school board could hold fear of firing over my head. They knew I had absolutely no fear of being dismissed.

You might examine how you can achieve the same inner confidence about your job. When you do, it's a potent source of strength and serenity that ultimately makes you a much better leader. You are not vulnerable to inappropriate pressure.

⇥ Promise Yourself ⇤

1. Promise to be so strong that nothing can disturb your peace of mind.

2. Promise to be as enthusiastic about the success of others as you are of your own.

3. Promise to be too large for worry, too noble for anger, too strong for fear, and too happy to permit the press of trouble.

⇥ Don't Cheat ⇤

If you are a lazy leader; if you are not willing to pay the price to go to clinics, conferences, and seminars; if you don't read all that you can; if you don't seek information from all sources; if you don't analyze those under your supervision as well as yourself (and then let yourself be governed by that analysis)—if you are not willing to do all these things—then you are cheating somebody.

You are not doing what you are being paid to do. No one else may know because in the final analysis you will be the only one who can reveal it.

Nevertheless, you are cheating. You are not doing your job to your fullest ability.

⇥ Why? ⇤

- Is it so much easier to give blame than offer credit?

- Is it that we dread adversity when we know that facing up to it makes us stronger?

- Is it so difficult to develop the belief that our team is working *with* us, not for us?

- Is it so much easier to talk than to listen?

- Is it that we often forget that big things are accomplished only by the perfection of little things?

- Is it that we aren't more interested in finding the best way rather than in having our own way?

- Is it so much easier to be a critic than a good example?

- Is it that we see the faults of others so much faster than we see our own?

⇥ Make No Mess ⇤

I did not believe in scouting opponents because it's a negative approach. (I do believe in having a *general* knowledge of the competition, which comes from knowing the background of the other coach.)

Our players had enough on their hands perfecting my system. Where would they have been if I had started teaching them how to react to every little thing the competition might or might not do? It would be a mess.

Let your competition figure you out. Let your competitors deal with the mess.

⇥ THE TEAM I ⇤ SCOUTED HARD

While I did virtually no scouting of other teams, I arranged to have our own team carefully scouted about three times a year.

Often you can't see the forest for the trees, and it's beneficial to have constructive criticism from outside neutral sources, to see your organization through the eyes of somebody else.

It is perhaps misleading for me to say I didn't scout teams. I scouted the most important team on our schedule: UCLA.

What measures do you take to have your own organization scouted? Keep in mind that scouting your team is just another way of scouting your own leadership.

⇥ PASSION'S SLAVE ⇤

Passion is cited as a prerequisite for success and high achievement. Not to quibble, but I view passion as emotional agitation—uncontrollable and overmastering.

Few would argue that the passion you feel when you're in love is wonderful. Few would deny that you are often irrational in that passionate state of mind.

How can irrationality bring success on a consistent basis (except perhaps when it comes to being in love)?

Passion is unsustainable over the long term. Success is a long-term process even when it's just 60 minutes on a clock above a basketball court.

For this reason, I never gave rah-rah speeches, never invoked the great urgency to "win" this or that game or "beat" this or that opponent. I never even permitted the players to charge out onto the court all fired up.

I didn't want them all fired up and jumping up and down. I wanted them bristling with intensity, finely focused, and in control of themselves.

When these attitudes are combined with talent and good teaching, you may find yourself leading a team competing and prevailing at the highest levels.

This will not occur if you are a slave to passion. Passion is temporary.

⇥ I Wonder ⇤

- Why are there so many who want to build up the weak by tearing down the strong?

- Why is it so difficult to realize that you cannot antagonize and positively influence at the same time?

- Why are we are so slow to understand that failing to prepare is preparing to fail?

- Why is it so much easier to complain about the things we do not have than to make the most of and appreciate the things we do have?

- Why is it that so often we permit emotion rather than reason to control our decisions?

❧ THE PROGENY OF WINNING ❧

It's true: Winning breeds winning. What people forget to mention is that winning also breeds complacency. My observation is that complacency is the more common offspring of winning.

❧ A LEADER'S DESTINY ❧

A leader destined for success asks, "What can we do to improve?"

A leader destined for failure says, "That's the way it's always been done."

Which are you?

—Anonymous

❧ GETTING THERE AND STAYING THERE ❧

Staying on top is very difficult, but not nearly as difficult as getting there. I believe this is true, in part, because you learn so much along the way. If you persevere and prevail, by the time you get to a position of dominance, you've accumulated a great body of knowledge and experience.

Additionally, the visibility you receive when you're on top can make your organization attractive to the best talent. Top talent coupled with leadership experience and knowledge is a pretty good hand to play. And that's the hand you've usually got when you're on top.

Of course, everyone is aiming at you at that point, but I'd much prefer to be the target than have it the other way around.

Staying on top is easier than getting there. Most of those in positions of leadership don't know this, however, because they've quit trying long before they reach the top.

⇥ THE EXPECTATIONS OF OTHERS ⇤

Usually when Hoosier friends visit me in Los Angeles, they want to see the homes of the movie stars. However, one fellow from Mooresville, Indiana, had a different request. "John," he said, "will you drive me out to see the Pacific Ocean? I've never seen an ocean."

We got in my car and drove to a bluff overlooking the Pacific on a beautiful sunny day. My friend got out of the car, walked to the edge of the cliff, and stood in silence for a while—hands on his hips, just looking out at the vast expanse of gently rolling waves sparkling in the sunlight for hundreds and hundreds of miles.

Finally, he turned and said to me, "John, it's not as big as I expected." I could only chuckle at his response. "Would you like see where Jimmy Stewart lives?" I asked.

As we walked back to my car, I turned for a last look before we drove away. I may be wrong, but the Pacific Ocean seemed unfazed by its failure to meet my friend's expectations.

There is a little practical lesson here on how silly it is to live and die on the expectations of others.

The next time you've worked hard, done your best, and still find that someone is unhappy with you, remember the Pacific Ocean. It too had failed to meet someone's expectations.

⇥ "You Let Us Down, Coach" ⇤

In 1975 UCLA captured its eighth national championship in nine years. (The previous year, 1974, UCLA was outscored by North Carolina State in a double-overtime in the semifinals. Before that loss, the Bruins had won seven championships in a row.)

At the final buzzer in 1975, a UCLA booster ran out onto the court and shouted, "Congratulations, Coach! You let us down last year, but we got 'em this time."

I had let him down—failed to meet his expectations—by not winning an eighth straight NCAA national championship the previous year.

The UCLA booster was like my friend from Indiana whose expectations about the Pacific Ocean had gotten out of hand.

⇥ Five Things to Share ⇤

1. Share the work.
2. Share the credit.
3. Share the enthusiasm.
4. Share the information.
5. Share the love, care, and concern.

⇥ No Leader Has ⇤
All the Answers

For a couple of seasons at South Bend Central High School, I instructed players on exactly what I wanted them to eat at home before a game: a vegetable, a small piece of steak, water, and some Jell-O. My goal was to be sure they ate something that would give them strength but that would also be very easy on the stomach. I didn't want them to get indigestion or become tired because of their pregame meal.

I later found out that one of our players—the most inexhaustible person on the team—never ate what I prescribed.

I was upset that he disobeyed and confronted him, "What *do* you eat before a game?" He looked down at the ground sheepishly and replied, "Coach, I eat plenty of chili and beans with lots of milk. That's all we can afford at home."

His pregame meal of chili and beans with lots of milk worked great for him. It was a little reminder that I didn't have all the answers.

This is a reminder most leaders need from time to time.

⇥ Make a Life ⇤

Wealth doesn't necessarily bring real happiness. It may provide things that bring momentary happiness, but they won't endure.

Sometimes we get so concerned with making a living that we forget to make a life. That's how families are lost—when we get sidetracked chasing money, or recognition, or other false trappings of success.

We have to make a living, but we also must make a life with our family. It's easy to lose sight of that when we start chasing money and its traveling companions fame and power.

I was paid $32,500 during my final year as varsity basketball coach at UCLA. You will probably not agree, but I was a wealthy man. I made a living, but I also made a life.

⇥ The Trappings ⇤
of Success

I drive a 1989 Taurus. It works just fine. Since I purchased my Taurus, many automobile dealers around Los Angeles have offered me fancier cars—free. I wouldn't have to pay a penny as long as I gave the car my endorsement by driving it. I have politely turned them all down.

Fancy things—cars or otherwise—have never meant much to me. Maybe it's because when I was growing up in Indiana, we were surrounded by families that worked hard on their farms and seemed content being able to feed the family and provide a home, some education—the good things. The same was true for Joshua Wooden and our family.

We worked hard, but we had a very good life—even without an abundance of the material things.

For whatever reason, that stayed with me. I never developed a taste for fancy living or all the trappings of success. My dear Nellie felt the same way.

Life can be just fine without them. Better, perhaps.

⇥ How to Fool 10,000 People ⇤

Basketball is the greatest spectator sport of all. The ball is the biggest, the arena is the smallest, and the crowd is the closest. Because they're up so close, spectators think they know the most, and they let you know it.

Abe Lemons, a basketball coach who like all of us got plenty of advice from the peanut gallery, once told me, "John, when you're in the huddle during a timeout, at least move your mouth up and down. That way the crowd will think you're doing some great coaching."

Abe wasn't far off the mark. Sometimes all you have to do is move your lips to fool the peanut gallery. However, in my own experience, if your lips are moving you better be saying something. And it better be something worth listening to.

⇥ Adaptability ⇤

My leadership style was originally rigid—rules, regulations, and penalties. This forced me to ignore human nature, extenuating circumstances, and ramifications. A good leader doesn't ignore these things.

I eventually started incorporating something else leaders often neglect: common sense.

Replacing many of my rules and regulations with common sense and good judgment didn't weaken my authority; it strengthened it.

⇥ How to Give Strength ⇤

Because of my advanced age, which is sometimes mistaken for advanced wisdom, I am often asked, "What can be done about the breakdown of ethics and behavior we see around us—corporate misdeeds, political scandals, the subversion of honest competition in sports?" If I knew the answer, I'd be rich.

What I do know is that we each have control of our own behavior, or should, and the principles we choose to abide by, or don't.

How do we keep others from doing bad things? Perhaps by properly tending to our own business—by running an honest shop—we exert the greatest power of all.

The greatest teacher of all, Jesus, taught by example. His words, as they have come down to us through the ages, are important. His example affects me even more deeply.

What to do about the wayward behavior and tattered ethics of others? Be true to yourself. Others are watching. Do your job the way you're supposed to do it.

You give strength by being strong.

⇥ An Honest Loser ⇤

Is there a difference between robbing a bank for money and breaking the rules to win? How can one be theft but not the other?

Ill-gained profit is no different from ill-gained victory. Neither means much except to a thief.

I'd rather be an honest loser than a dishonest "winner" and rather have an honest dollar than a false fortune.

You haven't won a thing when you have broken the rules to do it.

Character Is More Than Honesty

You can be as honest as the day is long and still be short on character. How? You can be honest and selfish, honest and undisciplined, honest and inconsistent, honest and disrespectful, honest and lazy.

For a leader, honesty is a strong start, but you can't stop there. There's more to character than just being honest.

Sometimes There's No Solution

A leader will occasionally do the right thing, and it will still turn out very wrong. In 1968 during the so-called Game of the Century between UCLA and Houston, I took Edgar Lacey out of the game because we had a disagreement on how to cover Houston's superstar Elvin Hayes.

Much later in the game I decided to put Edgar back in, but when I looked for him, he was sitting near the end of the bench. It appeared to me that he was almost disinterested in what was happening on the court—as if he didn't want to play or didn't care about the game.

Seeing this, I changed my mind and kept him on the bench.

Afterward, reporters asked me about this, and I told them what I saw: "Edgar gave me the impression he didn't want to play."

In fact, Edgar *did* want to play. He just didn't look like it. Unfortunately, in the heat of the game I had no way of knowing this.

When we got back to UCLA, Edgar came into my office and told me to tell reporters that I had been wrong. I couldn't do that because I had told them the truth, namely, that it appeared to me that Edgar didn't want to play.

I was sorry he was upset, and I could understand why he was displeased, but I wasn't going to retract what I said. What I said is what I saw—an honest statement.

Unfortunately, because I wouldn't publicly retract the statement and apologize, Edgar quit our team. If I had known this was going to happen, I never would have answered the reporter's question. But I had no way of knowing what my answer—an honest opinion—would do.

Sometimes there's no solution—only consequence.

⇥ Maximize Your Assets ⇤

I intensely dislike being judged on those things over which I have no control. Perhaps that's why I have a near-fetish about trying to perfect those things that are under my control. This concept is deep-rooted in my approach to competition. Here's a simple example.

I wasn't tall for a basketball player—less than six feet—but I was quick. I recognized that there was nothing I could do about my height disadvantage, so I worked on improving the asset I did have: quickness.

I made sure I was in the best condition possible so that late in the game I'd still be quick when others were slow. Basketball games are usually decided late in the game.

For good conditioning to mean anything, my feet had to be in good shape. I used a solution to toughen them up, and I put powder over the solution. I wore two pairs of socks—one thin pair and regulation sweat socks over them. I put the socks on carefully and laced and tied my shoelaces correctly.

Simply put, I maximized my asset to minimize my liability: I was in top condition, took care that my equipment didn't let me down, and toughened up my feet.

Any aspect of the game that was under my control received similar treatment.

As a coach I eventually learned to do the same. I worked very hard to perfect all things over which we had control and wasted little time stewing over other issues—those that were beyond my power to change.

⇥ UNDERDOGS HAVE MORE FUN ⇤

The most fun of all is when you're the underdog. That's when you're playing to win. When you're the big favorite, you're playing not to lose. It's much more fun playing to win.

When you are the underdog, don't feel sorry for yourself. Relish the opportunity it offers—the opportunity to play to win.

⇥ Your Legacy Is in the Cupboard ⇤

It was important to me that I didn't leave the cupboard bare. When I retired in 1975, my decision was made easier knowing that the returning players as well as those just coming in—David Greenwood, Roy Hamilton, Brad Holland, and Kiki Vanderweigh—were top student-athletes.

I felt in my own mind that UCLA would be a threat to win titles for the next three years after I retired and that it would continue to attract top talent. And I was correct. In fact, UCLA won the conference title in each of the four years immediately following my departure.

I believe a leader should, as much as possible, provide for the future of the team. How it does when you're gone is a reflection of how you did while you were there.

How can a leader with integrity just walk away and leave the cupboard bare?

⇥ Past, Present, and Future ⇤

Recently a young man asked me, "Are you afraid of death, Mr. Wooden?" Well, I had to chuckle because at my age—I was born in 1910—that could be a touchy subject. But it's not.

"No," I replied, "I have no fear of death because my life has been blessed in too many ways: my family, especially Nellie before I lost her; a wonderful, fulfilling life in coaching; all of my friends and acquaintances; and, except for bad knees because of basketball, good health. I've been given so much for so many years.

"But I also do not fear death because I know out yonder I'll be with Nellie again. But not until after death. I look back on my life with appreciation and out yonder with anticipation—although I'm not going to do anything to speed things up."

⇥ The Sum of Things ⇤

Perhaps you think that's an unusual way to conclude a book on leadership—reflections on life and death. Nevertheless, my words to the young man are relevant here. They go to the sum of things—my life so far—and the comfort I take in knowing what's ahead out yonder.

I *have* been blessed in too many ways, and one of the greatest blessings of all has been my profession: teaching, coaching, and leadership.

⇥ Happiness ⇤

"A day lived without doing something good for others is a day not worth living." Mother Teresa wrote those words—and I believe those words to be true.

Furthermore, it has been my experience that doing good for others brings great inner peace, even joy, especially when done without thought of getting something back in return. Expecting so much as a thank-you diminishes the joy of giving and helping others. At least it does for me.

There are many ways of doing something good for others. Teaching is one of those ways. As a part of good leadership, it's a powerful way of doing good for many others.

Perhaps that's why being a coach has delivered such happiness to my door. It has allowed me the opportunity to help others—not only in basketball but in their lives.

I took this opportunity to be a teacher, leader, and coach quite seriously. Leadership is a trust—a sacred trust in my opinion.

Honor it and you can find happiness, experience true inner peace, and find real joy.

⇥ My Perfect Day ⇤

If I could go back and pick one single day in my life—in sports—to live over again, my choice might surprise you.

It would not be that day in 1927 when our Martinsville High School basketball team won the Indiana state championship. Nor would it be any game I played as a member of the Purdue Boilermakers or coached at Indiana State Teachers College or UCLA.

Here's the day I would pick if I could go back in time: I would like to conduct one more day of practice in the gym.

Each day of practice was, by far, the most fulfilling, exciting, and memorable thing I did as a coach—teaching those under my supervision how to achieve success as members of a team.

"The journey is better than the inn," Cervantes wrote. The struggle, the planning, the teaching and learning, the seeking (which, of course, is the journey) surpass all else for me, including records, titles, or national championships.

The awards and acknowledgment, the final score, all have their respective place, and I do not discount them. But, for me, Cervantes had it right: My joy was in the journey.

Perhaps you might examine the source of your own happiness—joy. Is it in your journey or only in the prize, the inn?

⇥ The Goal and the Promise ⇤

I believe success comes to you as an individual and leader only when you acquire peace of mind, which is a *direct result of self-satisfaction in knowing you did your best to become the best you are capable of becoming.*

It sounds so simple: Give it your best; that is success. But it is not simple; it's very hard. Attaining success, as *I* define it, in leadership or anything else, is elusive, complicated, and extremely difficult. Thus, I created the Pyramid as a practical guide for achieving success and competitive greatness. Winning, however you define it, in whatever context you seek it, is a by-product of success.

For me, *success* comes before victory. It is the first priority, the great goal. You must make the absolute effort to bring forth your own potential and teach your organization how to do the same. This is the philosophy I adhered to for 40 years as a teacher, coach, and leader.

Seek success with all you've got, and you'll do just fine. Teach the same to those in your organization, and they, too, will have the tools necessary to achieve competitive greatness. That's my promise to you. I can make that promise because that's exactly the way I did it.

THE WAY OF WOODEN

ANDRE McCARTER
UCLA Varsity, 1974–1976
one national championship

No Secret to Perfection

There are no secrets in basketball—none. Everybody knows everything. Everybody has the same information. Coach Wooden just used the information better, taught it better.

In every area of the game there is a correct way, a perfect way, of doing it.

The Wooden system was to teach the highest form of execution of those fundamentals.

Everybody knows the correct form for shooting a basketball—balance, finger placement, arm extension, and the rest of it. The same applies to everything else: defense, dribbling, passing, blocking out, all of it. There's a perfect form for doing those things.

Coach Wooden's preparation and teaching were so good that he got the closest to the perfect form from his players—especially under pressure when it counted. That was the difference he had over everybody. And he accomplished it because he had such a high level of love and determination and energy that it's hard to comprehend.

He was trying to teach the perfect form, and we were always trying to do it our way—like kids who wear their parents down by asking over and over and over again. Pretty soon the parent gives in. Coach Wooden didn't give in when it came to fundamentals.

One day in practice with [Bill] Walton, I did this move—a superb move running down the court toward the basket and then passing the ball behind my back. Before Bill had finished shooting the shot, Coach blew his whistle, and I could hear his footsteps marching across the court at me.

Fancy play like passing behind the back, even in a scrimmage, was almost treason because we knew he didn't allow it. It wasn't the right way, the perfect form.

By the time he got up to me, Coach was so upset by what I'd done he couldn't talk straight; the words wouldn't come out, and he just kind of stammered and fumed at me. The whole team just fell out because it was so funny.

Well, I didn't think it was funny. It was a great move I had just done, and that night I got madder and madder as I kept thinking about it.

The next day I stormed into Coach Wooden's office to let him have it. He was very polite. "Well, Andre, come in, sit down. What's on your mind?" And I told him in no uncertain terms what was on my mind: "That was a superb move I got criticized for yesterday in practice!"

But he didn't fight me about my move. He agreed it was a great move, but then he said if he allowed me to do it, others who didn't have that skill for passing behind the back would start doing it. Pretty soon everybody would be passing behind their back. "Where would we be then, Andre?" he asked.

But this didn't satisfy me. I told him if other guys couldn't execute the move, that was their problem, not mine. Why should I be punished?

Then he started digging around in his desk looking through those notebooks and little three-by-five cards of his. Pretty soon he found what he was looking for and read it to me: "Andre, statistics show there's a 78 percent completion rate with a behind-the-back pass and a 98 percent completion rate doing it the correct way, the chest pass."

That took it away. I had no argument left when there was a 20 percent difference in completion rate. He won the argument without a fight. I couldn't wear him down. Nobody could wear him down.

Some critics say, "Wooden won because he always had the best players." They're wrong, but that explanation gives them solace.

Coach won five national championships with UCLA teams that had no superstar players like Bill Walton or Kareem Abdul-Jabbar. In fact, his first national champion team was the shortest to ever have won the title. How do the critics explain those five teams? They can't unless they understand the Wooden system—what he believed in and how he taught it. And what he taught us was to pursue perfection.

I'm one of the lucky ones. I got to learn the way of Wooden.

EPILOGUE

How do you know I really believe what I've written here in this book, namely, that I did not judge my *success* on winning or losing; that the quality of effort in pursuit of your potential is the highest standard, even before the "score"; that peace of mind counts most; that only *you* know if you are a success; and that success cannot be measured in material things such as trophies, titles, or money?

"Coach Wooden, how do I know you mean it—that you really believe these things?" Well, you don't. You don't really know for sure. But I do. I know for sure that what is written here is true to what I believe.

I also want to clarify that leadership is not the exclusive domain of men and that wherever I have used the masculine gender to describe a leader, I am referring to both women and men.

In fact, in watching basketball today, I believe some of the finest team play is demonstrated by women's teams— most of them coached by women. This is very pleasing for me to see because getting those under your supervision to work as a *team* is perhaps leadership's toughest task.

And finally, I wish to share a few closing thoughts from others on the subject of leadership. The Four Laws of Learning have been around for a long time: Explanation, Demonstration, Imitation, and Repetition. I like to tell people there are actually Eight Laws of

Learning: Explanation, Demonstration (your own example), Imitation, and Repetition, Repetition, Repetition, Repetition, Repetition.

So, at the risk of annoying you, let me impart five final maxims that have also appeared elsewhere in my writing and that are very meaningful to me.

The first comes from Henry Wadsworth Longfellow and fully describes the singular power of what I call *industriousness*—the first and perhaps the most important block in the Pyramid of Success:

> The heights by great men reached and kept,
> Were not attained by sudden flight.
> But they, while their companions slept,
> Were toiling upward in the night.
>
> —HENRY WADSWORTH LONGFELLOW

The second is an observation whose source is unknown to me but whose relevance is, I believe, especially strong in today's leadership climate where egotism seems to be rampant:

> Talent is God-given—be humble.
> Fame is man-given—be thankful.
> Conceit is self-given—be careful.
>
> —SOURCE UNKNOWN

The source of the third maxim is also unknown to me, but its author obviously understood the necessity of staying the course with what I call *intentness*:

The one who once most wisely said,
"Be sure you're right, then go ahead."
Might well have added this to it,
"Be sure you're *wrong* before you quit."

—Source unknown

The fourth and fifth are observations from two great philosophers that address the most important leadership quality of all. Without it I don't believe great leadership is even possible.

As Abraham Lincoln stated:

Most anyone can stand adversity, but to test a man's character give him power.

Leadership is power. How you handle that power—or how power handles you—reveals your character.

A leader must have many different personal characteristics to build an organization that achieves competitive greatness and success, but without character they all add up to less and less.

In the Pyramid of Success I included the values and qualities that I believe constitute character, including *friendship*, *loyalty*, *team spirit*, *condition* (physical, mental, and moral), and *self-control*.

A leader who has these values within will attract similar people—individuals of character. The fifth observation is from Ralph Waldo Emerson, who summed up what happens next:

The force of character is cumulative.

And that cumulative force under the direction of a skilled leader can become a power to be reckoned with.

My admiration for leaders is not based on their achievements. Rather, it is based on the quality of their leadership. Character is the most essential component of good leadership.

I wish you good luck on your own journey to achieve success as a leader. I also hope you will keep in mind this observation from Cervantes:

The journey is better than the inn.

Make each day of your journey a masterpiece.

ABOUT THE AUTHORS

⇥ JOHN WOODEN ⇤

Many consider John Wooden the greatest coach in the history of American Sports. He is revered and respected for both what he achieved and how he achieved it. As men's basketball coach at UCLA, his spectacular career is nearly impossible to fully comprehend—never a losing season; 10 national March Madness championships in 12 years, 7 of them in a row; 4 perfect seasons; an 88 game winning streak; and more. According to *Sports Illustrated*, "There's never been a finer man in American sports than John Wooden, or a finer coach." Wooden was named national Coach of The Year five times.

He has been called a "philosopher-coach" because what he taught transcended the basics of how to play the game and focused more on his bigger goal of teaching how to bring out your best, both on the court and in life. His philosophy of leadership including teamwork, ethics, and high performance was evident in his coaching and has found a great audience in corporate America.

Wooden began his coaching career at Dayton (KY) High School in 1932, where his record during the first year was 6-10, his only losing season in a 40-year career. He taught basketball and English for nine years at South Bend (IND) Central High School before transitioning to the college level for two years at Indiana State

Teachers College. In 1948 he and his wife, Nell, and their two children, Nan and Jim, moved to Los Angeles, where he had been hired to coach men's basketball at UCLA.

Early in his career, Coach Wooden developed a philosophy of performance which he called The Pyramid of Success. This philosophy included 15 personal qualities and values one needed to fulfill his or her own potential, both individually and as part of a team, to attain competitive greatness, whether it's in sports or business. Many leaders in corporate America including owners and managers of small businesses have embraced this philosophy and found it a valuable resource that helps their companies pursue and achieve top performance standards in the most competitive situations.

In 2008, the UCLA Anderson School of Management joined forces with Coach Wooden to create the John Wooden Global Leadership Award, which honors a corporate executive whose leadership and community service reflects the integrity, ideals, and standards of John Wooden. Past honorees include Howard Schultz (Starbucks), Robert Iger (The Disney Companies), Kenneth Chenault (American Express), Dr. Paul Jacobs (Qualcomm), Peter Ueberroth (Contrarian Group), Indra Nooyi (Pepsico), Federick Smith (FedEx), Ursula Burns (Xerox), W. James McNerney (Boeing). The 2017 honoree was Kevin Plank (Under Armour).

In 2004, Coach Wooden was awarded the Presidential Medal of Freedom for his lifetime of teaching, coaching, and leadership. Visit his official website: CoachWooden.com.

⇥ STEVE JAMISON ⇤

Bestselling author Steve Jamison has collaborated with some of America's greatest coaches including, Bill Walsh, creator of the San Francisco 49er's dynasty that won five Super Bowls; Brad Gilbert, Andre Agassi's coach during six Grand Slams; and the legendary John Wooden, with whom Jamison coauthored several best-selling books during a 15-year professional relationship. He served as executive producer for the award-winning PBS documentary, *WOODEN: Values, Victory and Peace of Mind*.

Jamison is considered America's foremost author and authority on the life and leadership of Coach John Wooden and serves as an advisor to the John Wooden Global Leadership Award.

Visit www.stevejamison.com for more information.